BETTER DAYS AROUND THE CORNER

First published in 2004 by Kachere Series
PO Box 1037, Zomba, Malawi

ISBN: 99908-76-05-3 (Kachere Text no. 17)

Distributed outside Africa by African Books Collective, Oxford, UK
www.africanbookscollective.com

Layout: Olive Goba
Photography: Jack DeJong
Cover design: Mercy Chilunga and Gladys Phiri

Cover photo: Boy up in the tree - Chisomo Chisaka
                 Girl under the tree - Pauline Kalampa
Special thank you to the Sacred Heart Community Day Secondary School, Zomba
for allowing us to take photographs of these two hard working students. And thanks
to the teachers: Mr. R.T. Kallawo, Mr. B.A. Chibwana and Mrs. M.M. Chikosa.

Printed by Lightning Source

Better Days around the Corner

Restoration of Hope, Self-Confidence and
the Desire to Succeed

Andy G. Khumbanyiwa

Kachere Text no. 17
Zomba
2004

Kachere Series,
P.O. Box 1037, Zomba, Malawi
email: kachere@globemw.net
www.sdnp.org.mw/kachereseries

This book is part of the Kachere Series, a range of books on religion, culture and society in Malawi. Other Kachere Books published so far are:

Janet Y. Kholowa and Klaus Fiedler, *In the Beginning God Created the Equal*

J.C. Chakanza, *Wisdom of the People: 2000 Chinyanja Proverbs*

Peggy Owens, *When Maize and Tobacco Are Not Enough: A Church Study of Malawi's Agro-Economy*

James N. Amanze, *African Traditional Religion in Malawi: The Case of the Bimbi Cult*

Steven Paas, *English – Chichewa/Chinyanja Dictionary*

Rodney Schofield, *Jubilee Reflections: Rich and Poor in Christian Perspective*

Peter G. Forster, *T. Cullen Young: Missionary and Anthropologist*

Fulata Moyo and Martin Ott (eds.), *Christianity and the Environment: Care for what you have been given*

The Kachere Series is the publications arm of the Department of Theology and Religious Studies of the University of Malawi.

Series Editors: J.C. Chakanza, F.L. Chingota, Klaus Fiedler, P.A. Kalilombe, S. Mohammad, Fulata L. Moyo, Martin Ott.

Contents

Introduction

ACKNOWLEDGEMENTS

I am indebted to many people. It is difficult to enumerate all of them one by one. For those inadvertently not singled out by name – please accept my sincere apologies. I am very grateful to my father, Mr. Grandson Morris Khumbanyiwa and my mother, Mrs. Melesi Khumbanyiwa (abiti Makuya) first and foremost for giving me life. Their love and encouragement continue to be a source of inspiration. My wife Evelyn and children – Kate, Linda, Edwin, Beatrice and Norma have encouraged me to put on paper the powerful thoughts and advice I share with them from time to time. This booklet is a direct response and challenge to their persistent reminders.

I am deeply indebted to my English Teacher at Malosa Secondary School, Ms. Kathleen Bromley (RIP) who paid my school fees in my final year, when my parents could not raise the required fees. If she had not come to my rescue at that critical moment, I shudder to imagine what would have become of me. To my friends, acquaintances, brothers, sisters, cousins, uncles, nephews, aunts and colleagues too numerous to be singled out, I say thank you all for your trust, encouragement and confidence. Through your trust and confidence, I have learnt to believe in myself.

This booklet is dedicated to my late maternal grand mother Mrs. Elian Makuya (RIP). She was over 100 years old when she died in 1997. I hope to live a long, happy and fulfilling life like her. She taught me many lessons. Some of the most fundamental lessons indelibly implanted in me include: always believe you will succeed; be a good steward of your resources and assets; earn your money; take courage in trying new things - even if you fail; learn from your successes and failures; trust in God....

Introduction

This book has been written primarily for Malawians. The message herein, however, applies equally to all poor people of the world beyond the borders of Malawi. There is pervasive poverty, unemployment, hopelessness, frustration, anger and desperation in the lives of most Malawians. These problems are huge. They leave most of us confused - with no clue as to what to do. There is need for serious and honest soul searching in order to get to the bottom of these problems. Only then can we stand a chance of finding answers to these and many other questions in our lives.

Every problem has a soft spot. The challenge however is to find the soft spots of our numerous problems. This book is meant to restore hope and encourage you, the reader, to take deliberate steps in your life that will improve your lot. The mini chapters in this book are meant to introduce the topics herein. But the contents are not exhaustive. Re-read the book as many times as you can. More important, use the contents of the mini chapters to challenge yourself, initiate self-assessment and debate within the family and the community. This can lead to value-addition. It can also add meaning to your life. You must however be ready to take action - now. Try new initiatives and approaches. Be adventurous.

Malawi is a rich country. We need not be a poor people. The poverty and the mood in the country can easily cloud this truth. In spite of the prevailing poverty and problems we must all think beyond the framework of our problems. We should not focus our thoughts exclusively on our current circumstances. Rather we should focus more on what the situation should be. We must embrace hope!

Malawi has one of the richest agricultural soils. In addition, the country is very beautiful with huge tourism potential. Furthermore the country has an abundant natural resource base. Above all Malawi has a very resilient and hardworking people. These are the ingredients for a rich country.

Observing the poverty situation in Malawi, one gets a feeling akin to watching a movie where a group of thirsty people is standing knee-deep in a spring of fresh water, yet the group is complaining about thirst. How long will it take this group of people to open their eyes and realize that they need not be thirsty - they are in the middle of plentiful fresh water? This book aims to provide some advice on the restoration of hope and how to bring about some meaning in the lives of the majority of poor Malawians. Like the group of thirsty people referred to above the advice contained herein can only be useful to those who are ready, open minded and willing to take decisive steps to improve their lives.

Nobody can live your life! You must be courageous and committed to take the destiny of your life in your own hands. Hopefully, this book will provide you with a new pair of lenses through which you can clearly look at the world around you and see what you have been missing and hopefully your fundamental role and place in that world. As a people we must have dreams, visions, aspirations, plans and goals.

We should be determined to achieve our desired goals even in the face of problems, stumbling blocks and constraints. We must learn to persevere and hang in there even when the going gets tough. Nothing of real value comes free of charge. We must be prepared to pay the price in terms of planning, action, discipline, perseverance and hard work. We must be prepared to work extra hard towards the attainment of our stated goals. All successful and rich people we see in our villages and cities are only ordinary people like us, who have learnt to exert extra effort in their chosen projects towards the achievement of their dreams and goals. You can be one of them.

The cumulative success stories, goals, wealth, accomplishments, dreams and values of individual Malawians are what define our national identity. It also determines the status of our Motherland among the peoples of the World. Today, Malawi is at a crossroads. It is a community of poverty-stricken, hungry, thirsty, bare-foot, half-naked and sick people. We need not be here. One can look in the average Malawian's eyes and see hopelessness, frustration, anger, emptiness and no clue of what to do. Due to many negative events happening around us mainly perpetrated by people we so much trusted, there is a lot of confusion, anger and distrust. The build up of such anger, frustration, distrust, confusion and tension is dangerous. We could be sitting on a time bomb. The sooner we address these problems, the better for us all.

Giving free food to the hungry and a few coins to the poor is perceived to be the norm in helping to restore hope and improve their livelihood. Herein lies the legacy of our poverty. The Chinese have a saying that translates into something like – "teach a man how to fish and he will never go hungry again..." Malawi has received massive amounts of financial and economic aid from the donor community for nearly four decades. There is very little to show for it. Precisely this is because we have been given the proverbial fish each time we have been perceived to be hungry.

The average Malawians' capacity to think and fend for themselves remains dismally low. Time comes in the history of every nation when the good Samaritans need to get the message loud and clear - enough is enough! Malawi does not need handouts anymore - what we require are the proverbial hooks, lines and fishing skills so that we as a people can do our own fishing. This will ensure that we should not go hungry again.

The Good Samaritan's help has kept us perpetually poor for a long time. We are fed up with their handouts and by extension; we are tired of bearing the burden of poverty. What's more, fisher folk will tell you, fish, which has been caught by yourself, is sweeter than the one, which is given to you, or the one you buy from the market. Furthermore, you gain respect in the eyes of the world as a people who are able to feed yourselves.

Since independence, Malawi has implemented various development programmes aimed at poverty reduction, socio-economic development and enhancement of the living conditions of its citizens. The on-going poverty alleviation programmes under the Malawi Social Action Fund (MASAF) is a multi million-dollar programme, jointly funded by the Malawi Government and a number of donors. Experts indicate that in spite of the massive amounts of money pumped in support of MASAF programmes and projects the poverty situation in the country continues to get worse. While MASAF programmes continue to construct bridges, maintain roads, construct classrooms, sink boreholes to provide potable drinking water, support poor farmers with farm inputs and many other commendable initiatives, the truth is that the poverty situation continues unabated.

The poverty situation in Malawi is a physical and exterior manifestation of a deeper and much larger interior poverty. Unless and until we begin to address the internal sources of the problem, no matter how much money is pumped into the on-going programmes and the construction of physical infrastructure, the poverty situation will continue to get worse. Clearly in terms of improving the livelihood and economic well being of the masses success rate so far is very limited indeed. As somebody once said, "failure is God's way of telling you – hey you are heading in the wrong direction..." If we are to change the economic fortunes of the majority of Malawians, we need to change course.

The attitude and mindset of the individual Malawian is the first port of call if we are to make an impact in the fight against poverty. Let each and every one of us make a commitment to change. But change what? Let us all have vision, mission and goal for our lives. Let us all devise plans, which we will follow religiously towards the achievement of our desired goals. Let us work hard. Let us persevere. In all our endeavours let us be honest and patriotic. There are better days ahead. The future is bright. Believe in yourself and your dreams.

John F. Kennedy, the former President of America, once challenged the American people not to ask what America can do for them but rather ask what they can do for America. We should do the same - stop thinking about what the Malawi Government and the donor community will do for us. Let us all join hands and commit ourselves to doing our utmost for the motherland. Let us be a productive people. We should endeavour to change our economy from mere consumption to a productive economy. Let us commit ourselves to change out fortunes from failure and poverty to success and wealth.

On your path to economic emancipation and success, there will be setbacks, failures and stumbling blocks. With a definite purpose in your life you must refuse to be discouraged. Your goal should serve as the torchlight that illuminates the way to your chosen destination. Be prepared to change course if it is absolutely necessary to do so but maintain your goal. The setbacks and stumbling blocks of our lives should be converted into stepping stones and springboards to propel us to higher levels of achievement.

Our forefathers and the heroes of our nation have written the first chapters of the history of Malawi. Their successes have been remarkable in many respects. They have to be commended. Through their efforts and hard work, today, we have freedom, democracy and peace. They have excelled in various areas of human endeavour including agriculture, politics, commerce, sports, entertainment, science, academia, journalism, civil service and many more. There is a lot of unfinished business. There is a lot more for us to do in order to ameliorate their achievements. More important, the remaining chapters of the history of Malawi have to be written by us, our children and great grand children. We should be prepared to leave an admirable legacy. The biggest challenge of our time is to transform our country and economy from poverty to wealth and from a consumer to a productive and industrial economy. This will add meaning to the lives of the vast majority of the citizens of Malawi and will be a major bonus to the prevailing freedom, democracy, peace and tranquillity. Thus more jobs and wealth will be created thereby contribute to putting food on people's tables and smiles on their faces.

The path to the transformation of our country's economy starts at the doorstep of each and every one of us. All hands must be on deck in order to achieve this mammoth task. Nobody should be allowed to sit on the fence. Let us all join hands by using our God given gifts, talents, skills and intellect to effect a change in our lives and the lives of all Malawians.

Fellow Malawians, let us think. There is no dignity in poverty! Every Malawian has a right to enjoy a minimum level of success and affluence measured with a Malawian yardstick. Each and every one of us has absolute control over our thoughts and minds. As many authors have stated, our thoughts determine our words. Our words determine our actions. Our actions determine our habits while our habits determine our character. Finally, it is our character that determines our destiny.

If our thoughts are completely focused on poverty we become a poor people. On the contrary if our minds and thoughts are fully focused and concentrated on success and wealth we become a successful and prosperous nation. Let all of us therefore commit ourselves to focus our minds and thoughts on success and wealth. Our thoughts are very important, as they are the factories where our destiny is defined and manufactured. There is light at the end of the tunnel. The future is bright for mother Malawi!

Chapter One

Poverty in a Land of Plenty

Malawi is a rich country. How such a rich environment should be steaming with poverty-stricken, hungry and half-naked people is beyond comprehension. The bottom line is that we are yet to wake up, open our eyes and realize the incredible wealth under our feet and within reach. As a people, we need to sharpen our imaginative and perceptive faculties in order to tap from the abundant resources and opportunities prevailing in our land. We need to take advantage of the abundant opportunities available in our midst in order to fight the grinding poverty.

Experts estimate that 70% of the people in Malawi are poor. About 2.8 million live in dire poverty. The question is why? Why is this the case in a country that has abundant natural resources, rich agricultural soils and hard working people? An attempt will be made in this mini chapter to touch on some of the fundamental and salient issues surrounding our poverty. This analysis will be helpful in the task of determining the strategic direction the nation ought to take, but more importantly what options individual Malawians should think about in order to improve their lot.

Indeed the question of how to eradicate poverty from our motherland should continue to occupy the minds of all of us. Many Malawians talk about poverty in abstract, derogatory and insinuating terms. The truth is that, poverty in Malawi is real, growing and a very serious matter. It is a subject, which requires all our intellect and hands in order to achieve lasting success. What can we do to eradicate this problem from our midst?

Donors continue to remind us from time to time about the poverty situation in Malawi. Besides, they even go further to prescribe what we should do in order to improve the situation. Some of their prescriptions have included downsizing, structural adjustment programmes, privatisation of government parastatal organizations, political pluralism and many wonderful pieces of advice. In spite of the good advice received and effectively implemented, we continue to be a very poor people. It may even be argued that in the course of following and implementing the expert pieces of advice from the donor community we have grown even poorer.

Nobody can deny that Malawi is potentially a very rich country. But again, nobody can deny that currently we are a very poor country. Indeed, we only need to open our eyes a bit wider and do certain things differently in order to make a difference in our socio-economic development. We have to move away from our national "comfort zones" in order to reposition ourselves for take-off. What are those things we need to do differently for the country to turn around? Hopefully, this book will help you to answer this question. But you must be ready and prepared for the advice herein, to have meaningful impact on your life. The book can only introduce a few ideas and provoke your thought process a little.

The challenge is for you to take the next steps required in order to change your situation from poverty to wealth. Please take the debate further. More important, extend the debate beyond mere words and lip service to a point where we are all ready for action. As a people we have not given adequate time and energy to holistically think through the question of poverty reduction in our motherland. Of course, the government has the responsibility to put in place supportive and responsive framework, strategies and infrastructure to support individual people's initiatives. But the major onus is on us the individual Malawians.

The debate about poverty reduction in the motherland should encompass a whole range of issues from social, economic, political and cultural dimensions. A lot of disjointed programmes have been implemented and volumes of lip service have been provided. Political rhetoric and empty statements have been the norm rather than the exception. This is particularly so as we get close to election time. But not much has changed over the last four decades, in practical terms.

The twin industries of agriculture and tourism hold the key to the nation's wealth and prosperity. The tourism potential remains untapped. The country has a rich, diverse and unique culture, ethnic groups, traditional dances, foodstuffs and natural resource endowment. With a breathtaking picturesque landscape, beautiful fresh water lakes, virgin beaches, beautiful plateaus, forest reserves, wildlife and fisheries the potential is unlimited. Malawi boasts one of the friendliest and smiling people on earth. Tourism industry has great potential for development and growth. All these factors make Malawi, potentially, one of the best tourist destinations in Africa. With a well-developed tourism industry, associated services will also develop thereby attracting more tourists and creating jobs and wealth.

Malawi has very rich agricultural soils. Agriculture has the potential to feed the nation, develop export trade and transform the country through development of agro-processing industries. We will look at the twin sectors of agriculture and tourism in a bit more detail in separate mini-chapters 9 and 10. Lake Malawi has many unique and endemic species of fish. *Chambo* is probably the best known and perhaps the most delicious fish on planet earth. Admittedly the lake and its resources are being poorly managed and over exploited. There is an urgent need to put in place a sustainable management and harvesting plan for our fisheries resources.

The country's major developmental asset is its smiling, resilient and hard-working people. Malawians have earned a reputation for their discipline, integrity, honesty and hard work. Whenever Malawians have ventured outside the country either for study or work, they have brought home admirable accolades of honesty, hard work, trustworthiness, diligence and dedication to duty. This is obviously good news. It is paradoxical that with such a hard working and disciplined people, Malawi should continue to be as poor as it is today. What has gone wrong?

Malawian young men and women have also done us proud in academic excellence. They have won prizes for exceptional academic performance both within and outside Malawi. These intelligent young men and women with their first class degrees/diplomas have returned home, integrated themselves into society and workforce without fully utilizing the knowledge and skills to bring forth meaningful changes to our society.

Our intellectuals have made little or no effort to make meaningful difference in creating wealth and jobs. They have not used their intellect to create goods and services to meet the needs of our communities. Indeed they have not yet innovatively found a niche for using their knowledge, skills, talents, gifts and experience to create wealth. They have come back home from their studies only to join queues of barefoot job seekers in our towns and cities. They are yet to learn how to invest in manufacturing thereby create jobs and wealth. They are yet to learn how to convert their newfound knowledge, skills, talents, and gifts into moneymaking machines and in the process create jobs for our brothers and sisters. If our intellectuals cannot create wealth and jobs for the nation, who will? Their counterparts from the developed countries return home from the same training institutions with clear ideas on how to create wealth and jobs, bring about new inventions and many new ideas. They return home with clear plans and ideas on the next steps to be followed. Why don't our brilliant young men and women also come back home from such courses and use their newly acquired knowledge, skills and contacts to undertake research and development towards new inventions and breakthroughs and create jobs and wealth? This is a million dollar question.

As a nation, we need to invest in the development of Malawi's human capital beyond mere reading and writing. There is need to challenge people's thinking, attitudes, values, perceptions, and imaginations. We need to develop the mindset, perceptive and imaginative faculties should also be developed. In addition, we need to enhance development of business acumen among the Malawian people. The individual's mind is every person's most important asset for achieving one's dreams and goals. The mind is a very powerful factory where your dreams and successes or failures are fabricated. To a large extent, as a nation we are not utilizing our minds and thoughts effectively and efficiently.

The building blocks of a country's wealth are the values, visions, dreams, goals, efforts, successes and wealth of the individual citizens. The primary point of intervention therefore should be at the individual level. Unfortunately, most of the interventions so far, have been at the macro-level. The oiling of the economic wheels has to be done at the micro level in order to have the desired impact at the macro level. This is one major area where as a country we seem to have missed the boat. Unfortunately we seem to continue to head in the wrong direction. One definition of insanity is if one continues to do the same thing in the same manner but expecting to get different and better results. We are behaving like a nation of insane people hoping that one day we will reduce the grinding poverty yet we continue on the same path that has yielded poverty all along.

When are we going to stop this vicious cycle of poverty? We are a poor people who have tried the same strategies for ages without getting better results. We must be insane to think that by continuing to implement the same strategies we will one day make a breakthrough and eradicate the poverty. Let us all agree that indeed we must change. That is the only way forward. The question is what exactly is it that we should change?

If we want to be wealthy and successful, different from the poverty situation, which we have, then let us engage our minds to ensure that we achieve that which we want. Let us try to change the way we do things in order to get different results. You may find yourself throwing your arms in the air in despair because you have tried many different things but have failed and you continue to live in dire poverty. You wish the situation changed for the better. But the fact is that no matter how much you wish, the situation will never get better. It is not a matter of how much wishing you do that makes a difference. You need to take action in the right direction in order to improve your lot. The right direction of course differs from one individual to another. You need to engage your mind and brain in order to identify the right direction for you.

Malawi has a paucity of mineral resources. Some of the available mineral deposits include coal, vermiculite, gold, diamonds, rare earth minerals and other trace minerals. There are also reserves of uranium, glass sands, asbestos, graphite, phosphate, gypsum, ceramic clays and gemstones. Uranium is a very highly priced mineral and if indeed the country has the said deposits, the country should move quickly to exploit the reserves to generate resources for national development. Malawi also has huge deposits of bauxite on Mulanje Mountain. To date we are still engaged in debate regarding whether or not the exploitation of the bauxite will impact negatively on the environment. Indeed the environment is very important and should be protected at all cost. It is however possible to mine the bauxite in an environmentally friendly manner. Detailed and professionally undertaken environmental impact assessment (EIA) can help to define a strict regime of mitigation measures to be enforced.

All the countries surrounding Malawi have well developed mining industries. It is incredible to imagine that in the midst of all these mineral rich nations Malawi should stand out as the only country without meaningful mineral deposits. This may indicate that we are not looking adequately for the valuable stones. The mineral resources are there, no question about it. It may well be that our experts are using blunt instruments in the search for the precious stones. Keep on looking guys and please find better instruments, one day you will find them. We are not using the right expertise, tools and equipment. We just have to be a bit more creative and try to use the right technology in our search for these minerals. Soon we will find them and as a nation we will take our rightful place as a mining nation.

The foregoing may give the impression that most Malawians have thrown up their arms and are not trying. On the contrary, they are trying hardest to extricate themselves from the poverty-stricken lives they live. The truth of the matter however is that most Malawians have and continue to try and they should be given credit for their effort. However it is also true that most Malawians give up quickly when they meet one problem or another. Most Malawians are also quick to get frustrated, confused and end up abandoning their projects when confronted with a problem. Problems in our daily lives are used to separate boys from men and girls from women.

If only we could learn to hang in there a little longer when faced with crises, Malawi would be a different place today. It is said that the darkest hour is just before dawn. Please heed this advice. When your problems seem to be most painful and unbearable, if you hang in there a little longer you will get the breakthrough that you want. As one travels the length and breadth of the country one sees serious manifestation of an extremely hard working people: in their agricultural fields (large as well as small-scale farms), in the few remaining companies, industries as well as offices.

There are many businessmen/women engaged in various business enterprises including making and selling *zitumbuwa, mandasi, malyolyolyo, mowa wa masese*, selling agricultural produce, fruits, operating private schools, groceries, rest houses, motels, cottages and bars (Chibuku, Carlsberg), cottage industries including weaving baskets and mats, making pots, carving, making hoe handles, consultancy firms, construction companies, non governmental organizations (NGOs), internet cafes, charitable endeavours, manufacturing of various items including maize flour and fabrics, import and export of various goods and services, vendors trekking to South Africa, Zimbabwe, Dubai, Europe and other far away places to buy merchandise for sale in the country, sportsmen/women, including football, basketball, volleyball, badminton, tennis, chess, musicians. These and many others provide evidence to demonstrate that Malawians are not simply sitting and watching their poverty grow. They are undoubtedly trying hard.

While the list highlighted above is impressive, it must be said that the production and manufacturing sector in the country is still in its infancy and quite weak. Malawi is a net importer of manufactured products but an exporter of primary agricultural commodities. There are various opportunities for production and manufacturing, which have potential to create jobs, wealth and import substitution. Agrobusiness provides the greatest potential. There is need for the country to encourage more processing and value addition of the traditional export commodities so as to fetch more foreign exchange. In addition, the country needs to invest in industrial development.

Some of the plausible reasons why Malawi continues to be poor include ineffective government policies, inexistence of an enabling environment, a non-responsive educational system, brain drain (our best brains are being lured out in search of greener pastures), no culture of goal setting and prioritization, a pull him/her down (PHD) culture, corruption in high places, politics of poverty, survival and patronage and absence of a conducive environment that rewards hard work, efficiency, innovation and diligence. These are some of the cancers of our nation and enemies of our development efforts.

Chapter Two

The Desire for Success

Success by nature is quite elusive. This explains why we do not have multitudes of wealthy and successful people in our midst. Successful and wealthy people are few. It is only a handful of people that discover the magic formula. These successful people take the necessary steps to become wealthy and successful. They have what it takes to be successful and prosperous. Some of their characteristics include positive attitude, hope, faith, vision, perceptive mind, dreams and capacity to set goals, the courage to try new ideas, determination and perseverance.

If you want to be successful the initial stage is to have a very strong desire for success. If you want to be wealthy, the first step is to have a strong desire for wealth. Very simple, isn't it? Your mind and thoughts must be focused on success and wealth so intensely that they are not easily distracted. This desire should be very strong. As many writers have stated, what your mind can conceive and believe, you will achieve.

Success and wealth do not come by chance or good luck. There is no such thing as good luck. Meaningful success comes as a result of strong desire, determination to succeed and effective planning. Those who succeed have a strong desire to become what they want to be in life plus a very strong determination to do whatever it takes to achieve their dreams come rain or sunshine. It takes dreaming, planning, failure, doubt, fear, determination and persistence to achieve the desired goal. You must live your life in a way that you do not just constitute statistics. You should not just be one of the Malawians. You must be "the Malawian". You must have a distinctive adjective attached to your name.

Remember - everybody fails once in a while in life but successful people learn important lessons from their failure and take corrective action and move on to achieve their desired goals. Successful people refuse to be discouraged by temporary setbacks on their paths to success. Poor and unsuccessful people, once they fall down they refuse to wake up and apparently they enjoy the sympathy they receive from bystanders.

With adequate money in your pocket you can afford to buy the food you need to feed your family. You can afford three square meals a day. You can even afford to give your children snacks in their school bags to take during school break. You can also afford to eat chambo and chicken on your table whenever you want. You can also afford the best medical treatment money can buy. You can even afford the best education for your children. With abundant money you can send your children to the best schools in the world with a view to equip them with quality education and skills, which can convert them into useful citizens of Malawi, and the world.

Let us face it, rich men/women are able to fend for their spouses and can afford to buy them the most expensive clothes and in return they receive abundant love, compassion, care and attention. Their families are bound to be happier. With peace of mind associated with success and wealth, the rich man/woman is able to think and plan clearly for more achievements and success. Success and wealth indeed can give you a sense of power, peace of mind and freedom of choice.

When you achieve success and wealth, you can afford to donate to charitable causes thereby enhance your status in society. Through philanthropic activities you can contribute to bringing smiles to orphans, widows and other members of society who are not well endowed. Money therefore increases your area of influence. People will associate with, trust and identify with you. With money you can do many things. While money may not solve all mankind's problems, it is true that it makes life comfortable and enjoyable. Money makes you happy and comfortable.

Without money and adequate material resources, you are nobody. You cannot even have adequate influence on your children's upbringing. If you cannot even provide for their daily needs, the children are likely to end up engaging in anti-social activities in order to get some financial resources with a view to make ends meet. Without money you cannot manage to provide for the needs and wants of your spouse. Suffering therefore becomes your lot.

If success and wealth is your goal, you have to put your body, soul, and mind into whatever you choose to do and be. Be committed to do the right thing always. You must have the courage to do the difficult things until your dream is realized. Success means a lot of good things in life. It means personal prosperity, peace of mind, beautiful home, financial security, good education for your children, and a lot more.

Obviously most of us are worried about our basic needs of food, clothing, shelter, protection and a sense of belonging. Successful people are not worried about such basic needs. With abundant material and financial resources at their disposal, the basic wants and needs cease to be problems. Their money solves most of their basic problems. With abundant wealth, the requirements and needs of the rich man/woman shift to a completely different pedestal. The rich man wants to travel to far away places, s/he wants to drive the most expensive car, s/he wants to buy the most expensive clothes and perfumes for his/her spouse, and wants to eat in the most expensive restaurants, drink the most expensive wines and many more things which are beyond the imagination of the poor.

In your search for success please remember the advice given by Zig Ziglar in his book titled "You Can Reach the Top". He writes, "money will buy a house but not a home; a bed but not a good night's sleep; pleasure but not happiness; a good time but not peace of mind; a companion but not a friend". Also take heed of advice given by Vash Young in his book titled "A Fortune to Share". He states in part "It is often that the man who pursues the dollar too diligently finds it hard to catch, but if he pursues other and better goals, dollars come around to see what sort of fellow he is." We need to engage our imaginative and perceptive mind to provide goods and services that are required by our communities and beyond. In the process of providing such useful services, dollars will come round (in our pockets) to see what sort of fellows we are.

Just look around you, you will see great differences in the life styles of those who are successful and rich compared to those who are poor. Those who are rich drive expensive cars, live in expensive mansions, put on beautiful and expensive clothes; their children are well fed and go to good schools. They also have businesses or professional jobs, which bring them large sums on a regular basis. The poor man/woman is poorly fed and cannot afford even a bicycle; children are poorly fed and dressed in tattered clothes. Even with free primary education introduced by the government, the poor families are still finding it extremely difficult to take full advantage because they cannot afford to buy school uniforms, pencils, erasers, pens and note books which the child requires for his/her schooling. Even with free education, the children do not want to go to school naked. Unfortunately, the poverty is handed down from generation to generation.

The advice I can offer here is that if you are a cleaner, be the best cleaner. If you are a clerk, be the finest clerk. If you are a cook, be the best cook. If you are a manager, be the best manager. If you are a husband, be the best husband and father. If you are a wife be the best wife and mother that you can be. If you are president, be the best president. These are some of the fundamental ingredients for success. Your mind is a very powerful asset that should be used to the full as you scale your way towards the attainment of your stated goals. It has been estimated that an average man or woman uses only about 5% of his/her mind's potential. This says volumes about each and every individual's potential.

There is unlimited opportunity in the utilization of your mind. Your mind is available for you to use to achieve wonderful results. Your mind is the only thing that you have absolute control over. If well utilized your mind can determine your destiny. You are entitled to use your imaginative and perceptive faculties to explore, dream, imagine and take necessary action to achieve your dreams. Be adventurous.

Do not limit your imagination, thoughts and dreams to the ordinary stuff. Remember, after all your dreaming, imaginations and exploration by the mind – take action. You will never know the beauty of success if you continue endlessly in your dreams, imaginations and wishful thinking and never take action. You will never know how to swim by standing at the edge of the swimming pool, planning how you can do it while watching other people swim. You must jump in the swimming pool, mix with those expert swimmers and use those beautiful ideas you have gotten during your planning and observation.

If your goal is to be wealthy and successful, here you are – your mind is there for you to use. You will never get rich by standing there merely observing what wealthy people do and planning how to become rich. Take action. Of course, every individual should dream about what s/he wants his/her circumstances to be. All of us have one problem or the other. But this should not cloud our thinking and dreams. In our dreams we should see what we want our circumstances to be and not what the current circumstances are. Our thinking should transcend beyond our existing situation and problems. We should focus our energy on what the situation can be and should be. And what we need to do to improve the situation. After this analysis move quickly to the most critical stage which requires you to take decisive action towards achieving your desired goal.

An important piece of advice - please open your eyes wide open and look around you critically and attentively. If you spend time thinking about these issues, you will soon identify opportunities and possibilities that are available to you. You will clearly pinpoint ideas and opportunities, which can make a difference in your life. In the process of implementing your identified opportunities you will fill a vacuum, which will also make you feel happy. More important, you will make a few Kwachas and Dollars for yourself. This idea will be elaborated further in mini chapter 5.

Start from where you are. If you are sincere and objective, you will not have long to look. The answer will hit you in the face quite quickly. You will even wonder why you have not seen such opportunities all these years. It will be obvious things and circumstances, which have always been there. In fact one important area to look is your own gifts, talents, skills, hobbies and interests. Those things which you enjoy doing can provide answers and point you in the direction of your success and wealth.

If you want to be rich and successful, the idea highlighted above should get you thinking deeply in terms of how you can convert your gifts, talents, skills, passions, likes and hobbies into money-making machines. What a wonderful world it would be if all of us were engaged in careers and/or businesses, which are in conformity with our passions, skills, gifts and talents.

However, if you have not yet discovered your passions, skills, gifts and talents do not lose heart. Look around you. Critically analyse needs, wants, challenges and problems, which are causing people to have sleepless nights. Every human problem has a solution. Are there any of such needs, challenges and wants that you can help to solve? Can you use your God-given talents, gifts, skills, knowledge to ease the pain, suffering and want? It is in the search and provision of solutions to your neighbour's problems that will keep you busy. It is your help that will bring happiness and smiles on the faces of your neighbours. In the process your pockets will be bulging with plenty of cash, as your neighbours will obviously pay you for the goods and services you will provide.

The hungry people need food –yes? Is there any way you can supply the food in your neighbourhood more competitively? People with bare feet require shoes. Sick people need medicine. Thirsty people need water. Jobless people want jobs. There is a long list of problems, needs, wants, constraints and challenges. The challenge for you, the reader, is to find solutions to these problems in a more competitive and economically friendly manner. You are never too young or too old to take on these challenges. You will provide essential service if you can ease the national problems of joblessness, poverty, industrial development, agro-processing, tourism development, agricultural development, declining standards of education, and many more. Easy isn't it? Start now and it will provide answers to the grinding poverty in Malawi.

A strong desire for success and wealth can do the magic for you. With the desire indelibly printed in your mind, you need to set specific goals in accordance with your purpose in life. In addition you should set up a plan that will specify how you intend to achieve your desire. Having clearly set out your plan, please work hard. You are surely on the right path towards the achievement of your goal. There is no substitute for hard work. When you face problems persevere and hang in there.

It is essential to pose, plan and strategize on how you are going to reach your goal; what exact activities you are going to undertake to achieve your goal; what are the required inputs; what intermediate steps, you need to achieve before you achieve your major goal; who are the people you will need to consult or to work with you in achieving your dream; how long will your dream take to accomplish; can the dream be broken down into short, medium and long term accomplishments; where do you need to begin; what financial resources are required; whose advice do you require before you start and many other considerations.

Please take action once you have clearly defined your plan and found answers to these questions. If you wait for all the problems to be resolved before you start, you will never get started because there will always be problems in this world. Problems will continuously militate against your best ideas and plans. Be courageous and adventurous enough to try new ideas and innovative ways of doing things.

The progressive achievement of your short-term and medium-term goals defines the rate of your success towards the attainment of your long-term dreams. After you have drawn up your plan – the road map for your success - take action quickly without delay. The right time to take action is NOW. If you wait until you have enough money, forget it. You will never have enough money. If you wait until you are old enough you will never grow old enough to start your project.

Review your plans critically in the light of the existing circumstances and where necessary revise your plans taking into account new realities. But never quit. Successful people never quit and quitters never succeed. A strong desire to be successful and wealthy is an important and critical attribute you need for you to be successful and accumulate riches. Behind the desire to be rich, you must have a specific dream. Your dream should be backed by strong determination to succeed. Strong determination that does not recognize failure!

The vast majority of Malawians are poor because they have accepted poverty as their lot. Most Malawians have given up the fight to extricate themselves from poverty. They have not developed a strong desire to be wealthy. Most Malawians have what it takes to be rich and successful - powerful brain, mind, body, education, training, talents, gifts and skills among others. Most people have tried a number of projects a number of times but they have failed. As a result they have come to the conclusion that it is impossible to succeed in Malawi. This conclusion printed in their minds is the root cause of their poverty.

The notion that something is impossible poisons the whole mind. It is important for us all to learn to draw positive conclusions from whatever circumstances we find ourselves in. We can never change the circumstances that occur in our daily lives. But we can control the way we respond to the occurrences and the lessons we draw there-from. Indeed every successful person has faced problems and failed. All of us will fall down from time to time on our chosen path to success. But you must learn to wake up, dust yourself, learn how not to fall down again and move on every time you fail.

All of us have experienced in our daily lives, situations when we said to ourselves, "I will do this". The results have almost always been wonderful. I recall early in my career, I had problems with my boss. I also had problems coping with my new job. I also had problems comprehending the rules and procedures. Instead of addressing these challenges I labelled my boss - difficult. This is common to many of us. I even got an impression that my boss was all out to embarrass me or make life difficult for me. Even the idea of quitting crossed my mind. Most of you will identify with these feelings.

One day, while reading a book titled *Think and Grow Rich*, I got the following advice: "winners don't quit and quitters don't win". This made my day! I resolved there and then to be a winner and never to quit. I also decided that I was going to study the rules, procedures and regulations of the institution and avoid all the embarrassment I was facing from time to time. I promised myself that each and every assignment given to me would be undertaken with absolute care, accuracy and to the best of my capability. The result of this personal counsel and rebuke has been wonderful and rewarding. Try it. If it worked for me, it can work for you too.

Remember there will always be temporary setbacks. These are only temporary. Persevere until you achieve your goal. Wealth awaits those who are strong and determined enough to acquire it. The first step is your own thoughts and determination to become successful and rich. Nobody can make that decision for you. That decision and determination must be very strong that no matter how much setback and opposition you face your determination should carry the day.

For you to achieve success, you need to attain a certain degree of self-discipline. Discipline unlocks the doors to success, accomplishment and the accompanying feeling of satisfaction. Discipline requires that you do the right thing at the right time, in the right manner and right magnitude. Discipline is the foundation on which success is built. If your goal requires that you grow 25 ha of tobacco, please grow 25 ha of tobacco, if not more. If you grow 8 ha only, you are on your way towards failure.

If you decide that you want to stop smoking and you keep stocking your home with packets of cigarettes, obviously you are planning to fail. It is said that failure to plan is akin to planning to fail. If your goal is to stop excessive beer drinking and you continue to visit your usual drinking joints then I am afraid you are courting failure. If you have decided to save 20% of your net salary every month and you end up saving only 5% obviously the results will not be as desired. If you are overweight and have decided to lose 20 kg and this requires that you reduce your food intake, run 2 km every morning and go to the gym for work out 2 hours every evening. That is the discipline required for you to achieve your goal. There is need for discipline in order to ensure that you do not go back to your old habits. Discipline is very important for anyone who wants to succeed in life.

We all know how difficult it is to wake up early in the morning to go to work, to the garden, to the market or to do whatever you want to do. The bed is just too comfortable in the morning. Many people fail to achieve their dreams because they fail to discipline themselves to leave the bed at the right time in the morning. In so doing they miss important opportunities, which could have made a difference in their lives. It is important to appreciate the importance of discipline in one's chosen path to success.

Ask yourself what exactly you want to be in life; what exactly you need to do in order to achieve your goal; what are necessary adjustments you require to make in your life in order to achieve your goal. Are you willing to make the necessary changes required in your life's routine in order for you to attain your goal?

Are you willing to maintain the requisite discipline and to do the needful and right things consistently in order to attain your goal? It does not help you to maintain discipline today only to change your mind tomorrow. Your commitment to self-discipline will be tested when problems occur. Make a commitment to keep on doing the right thing even when you experience some problems. Opportunities come to those who are disciplined and have developed the skills of self-control and the ambition to be what they want to be. Self-belief is very important as it helps you to develop a sense of determination, which is required for the achievement of your dream. Systematic planning and strategizing makes it easier for you to achieve your desired goal. If you plan to build a house and you achieve your goal, the level of your self worth and confidence rises. You will say to yourself, "if I can build a house of my dream, then I should also be able to buy that car I have always wanted!" Then once this happens you are on the right path towards achieving success. The successive achievement of seemingly simple objectives/goals one after another add up to a successful life.

Self-confidence is what you need to carry with you as you scale your way through to the high echelons of success. Let me emphasize that it has nothing to do with education. In fact most of our highly educated people in Malawi are more attuned to white-collar jobs and more often shy away from taking up powerful challenges that have potential to improve their lot, generate wealth and create jobs in our poverty stricken land. Arguably, this is one clear legacy of the malaise in our education system. Some of the richest men in Malawi are school dropouts. One such man is Felix (not real name). Felix dropped out of school at the age of 13. He decided that he wanted to be successful and wealthy. He did not like school very much. In spite of his parents' insistence that he should go back to school, he refused.

He stayed at home for about one year in which he tried to think of what to do and how to achieve his dream of being successful and rich. Finally he decided to go into business. He did not have money and no clue of what business he wanted to go into. After some months of quality thinking he decided to go into business selling roasted peanuts. He asked his mother and father for seed money but both refused on account that he had refused to go to school. In fact his parents insisted that even at that stage he ought to go back to school. He asked all his uncles, cousins, aunts, nephews, nieces, grandparents and friends. None could help him. Eventually he decided to help himself.

After maize harvest it is a tradition in my village that children go to the fields and pick whatever the harvesting crew may have left behind. This is called *kuvutula*. Felix joined his fellow boys and girls in the fields. While the other boys and girls had the goal of "shining" at school with the extra money generated, Felix had a powerful goal. The money he got from this transaction was invested in his business. He bought the first consignment of peanuts, a roasting pan, some salt, and containers with which to carry his wares to the market as well as a spoon for measuring out the peanuts during sale.

After three years in this business he accumulated enough money, which enabled him to start a second hand clothes business, commonly known as *kaunjika*. He operated this business for another four years and thereafter opened a one-hectare tobacco plot. Within five years his tobacco plot had become a 30-hectare farm. In the 80s and early 90s when tobacco prices were very good he made a lot of money. Today he is a rich man.

The question to you is - do you have a strong desire to be successful and wealthy? If the answer to this question is a firm yes – you are in the right direction. In other words those who are reeling in poverty not only have they decided to be poor but in addition they have lost the will and determination to succeed. It sounds cruel to suggest that the poor are poor because they want to be poor. However, if they want to turn their fortunes around and believe with their hearts and minds that they can do so, they will. The road to success is littered with huge obstacles and temporary set backs. Those who succeed are patient and

skilful enough to turn the obstacles and stumbling blocks into stepping-stones to propel them to higher levels of success. Setbacks and
stumbling blocks scare the weak-minded.

Chapter Three

Education and Training

Education and training can open up a whole range of opportunities and possibilities for an individual and a nation to succeed. If well-organized and managed education and training can ameliorate and sharpen inherent skills, talents, gifts, attitudes as well as perceptive and imaginative faculties. Unfortunately for most African Countries including Malawi education and training simply imparts skills in reading, writing and counting. To survive in the world we all need far more than reading, writing and counting!

The improvement in education and training holds the critical key to the development of Malawi. The education system in the country bears the hallmark of a colonial legacy. During the colonial era it is conceivable that the colonial masters may have devised an education system for individuals to get educated and trained to acquire minimum skills to enable them better serve the master. The system does not seem to have been structured to challenge the student's attitude, imagination, perception, skills and talents. Unfortunately, this state of affairs has continued to this day. It is therefore true that our education system is not responsive to the contemporary challenges in the 21st century.

Today's challenges require far more skills than mere reading, writing and counting. These skills may have served us well during the 18th and 19th century. Unfortunately our education system continues to graduate greater numbers of students whose outlook is limited to the basic skills of literacy and numeracy. There is therefore a sharp mismatch between the prevailing challenges and the capacity to deal with them. No wonder we are where we are. We must change course if we are to make an impact in our fight against poverty and in our efforts towards socio-economic development in Malawi.

It is estimated that about 30% of the Malawi's population is illiterate. These people are unable to read and write. Although free primary education was introduced in 1994 the education system is beset with massive problems ranging from low funding, inadequate and poor classrooms, high student: teacher ratio, poorly trained teachers, overworked but poorly paid teachers, inadequate teaching materials and high school drop out. These and other problems limit the chances for success of the universal free primary education in our country.

At the primary level, the combined effect of poor quality education system and classrooms leads to a drop out ratio of about 17%. Indeed about 50% of the pupils drop out before they can reach fifth grade and most probably, before they can attain sustainable literacy. Primary school completion rate is very low. Only 30% of the pupils who enter class one (1) complete primary school (class 8). Progression to secondary education stands at 18%. And only 0.3% of learners of eligible age gain entry to University. This is sad.

There is strong argument for improving the literacy rate both quantitatively as well as qualitatively. While all efforts must be made to ensure that the free primary school education succeeds and that all Malawians should have the opportunity to get educated, there is even a greater need to invest massive resources in improving the quality of education. This will ensure that our graduates have the requisite skills and capabilities commensurate with the challenges at hand.

We need to review the curricula at all the various education levels to ensure that the individual student's inherent skills, talents, gifts, attitudes, imagination and perception are identified, nurtured and developed. Effort should also be made to improve teacher training programmes, provide adequate teaching materials and provide adequate and good standard of classrooms, provide appropriate teachers' accommodation. Our teachers are not well paid. We need to remunerate our teachers adequately in order to motivate them. As a country, we also need to provide appropriate incentives for our teachers. Other issues to be addressed include improvement of the teacher: student ratio, enhance teaching-learning environment, reduce drop out ratio among others.

The current education system does little to challenge and empower the student. In addition it does not instill business acumen and positive attitude towards life's challenges. The education system is not serving us adequately. There is adequate justification to overhaul the education and training system in the country. The system should challenge the students and empower them with requisite skills and attitudes to enable them better survive in the real world. Graduates will therefore be able to add meaning to their lives and improve their livelihoods. They will also not rely completely on government and institutions to create jobs. On the contrary they will be able to engage in various business and productive activities, which in turn will generate wealth and create jobs for the country.

It may also be argued that in the current education and training system, the student passively participates with little or no input. A rehabilitated education and training system should provide for the student to be actively involved in determining the pace and depth of the system if s/he is to get the maximum benefit. It should not be a one-size-fits-all. The system should allow some flexibility to accommodate the individual skills, talents, gifts, manual dexterity and other unique characteristics. It is important for the student to be challenged.

Education and training should encompass a whole complex mix of aspects including reading, writing, counting, art, sports, music, gymnastics, debate, social issues, civics, politics, religion, attitudes, talents, skills, value systems, the relationships and interactions between and among parents, students, relatives, friends, acquaintances, fellow students and teachers among others. In other words education and training in a holistic sense.

In the course of implementing such a revised education and training system there is need to keep an eye on special talents, skills, attitudes, gifts, sportsmanship, idiosyncratic tendencies, comportment and other characteristics in the students. These should be nurtured and developed. They can provide a guide as to the individual student's role in society. We need to overhaul our curricula and education system so that we can get a responsive, practically oriented and holistic curriculum and education system. This can have an important impact in the transformation of our country. Our teachers have to be retrained in order to be able to effectively deliver the new curriculum being advocated.

The free primary education introduced in 1994 has added tremendous pressure to an already poorly funded education system in the country. While the goal is laudable, if the problems facing the system are not resolved, the results will be far from desirable. It is worth noting that since 1994 due to the introduction of free primary education the total enrolment in primary schools now stands at more than 3 million. Every year about 77,000 students are selected to enter secondary school education. In addition, only about 1000 students enter university/colleges each year. Due to the inadequate places in secondary and tertiary education there are lots of intelligent young men and women who are forced to drop out of school. Whether by design or default the education system leaves hundreds of thousands of idle people on the streets. Unfortunately our education and training system does little to prepare those who cannot continue with education with requisite skills and attitudes required in the real world. Does it surprise us that the rate of crime and homelessness is on the rise?

An idle mind is a workshop of the devil. There is need for both Government and the private sector to invest in secondary and tertiary education to take care of the demand created by the free primary school education. There is also need for creative thinking to equip the school drop outs with skills, talents and attitudes that can help them create and maximize the prevailing opportunities in the country by taking full advantage of their skills, talents, passions and other God given gifts.

It is a fact that in Malawi, most of the wealthy are school dropouts. Why is this the case? This may be an indictment on our education system. Why is it that our educated people who have read and travelled widely do not capitalize on what they read and what they see on their international travels to become wealthy and successful? Does our education system and employment conditions really equip the educated man and woman with the requisite tools to be able to make them successful and wealthy? In most cases the answer is a resounding NO. One would have expected our elite especially those who graduate from Business Administration School to be the best businesspeople and those who graduate from Agricultural Colleges to be our best agriculturists.

On the contrary our graduates are happy to go into blue and white-collar jobs. Running businesses and agricultural enterprises are left to people who have never seen the inside of a college lecture room. Cost-benefit analyses, profit and loss accounts and sensitivity analyses conducted by our elite would probably show that most business ideas are not viable. Yet the school dropouts use their intuition, to implement those very same ideas and prosper. Probably our education system imparts negative attitudes, which scares the elite from venturing into business. Something should be done quickly to address this aspect?

Each and every individual is unique. All of us have special skills, attitudes, passions and talents. God made you as a special person. There is nobody in the whole world who is like you. You are a special human being. You have unique skills, talents, gifts that are special.

Those special characteristics are the starting point on your journey to success and prosperity. This is particularly important for parents and teachers to note.

Usually parents tend to compare performance of their children against each other. In addition parents tend to encourage their children to follow career paths of interest to the parents. It becomes prestigious for the parents to brag that theirs is a family of doctors, architects, engineers, accountants and what have you! It is essential to recognize that while they are all your children, they are different people and may have different IQ, skills, gifts, passions, attitudes and talents. These individual characteristics should be identified, nurtured and developed. This is the challenge that both parents and the education system should grapple with.

By the time a pupil leaves primary school either to go to secondary school and onward to college or into the world, s/he should have an idea about his/her abilities, talents, skills, intellectual prowess and many other pointers. This will enable him/her to focus on his/her particular passion and talents for a career. In addition, it is necessary that the revised curricula and education system should introduce business management at all levels.

Wouldn't it be nice and wonderful if every person's career were linked to his/her hobbies, interests, talents and skills? It would not only be exciting but each one of us would enjoy our various jobs and/or businesses. This would lead to maximum productivity. The vast majority of people are engaged in jobs that are at variance with their interests, hobbies, skills, passions, gifts and talents. They are engaged in these careers simply because there are no other job opportunities around. As such the level of productivity is far below potential. There is also a tendency for children to go into careers that are forced onto them by pressure from parents/families. This does not provide the right environment for growth and development of inherent skills, talents, hobbies and capabilities.

Our schools also do not provide a conducive environment for teaching and learning. In a typical primary school classroom one finds pupils that are good in science, mathematics, art, languages, history, sports, manual dexterity and so forth. Due to lack of proper training and skills the teacher tries hard to impose a "one size fits all" strategy, where all students go through a similar programme of tuition with little or no regard to their inherent skills, talents and capabilities. It is futile to try and make all of them good mathematicians, historians or scientists. The result is that we end up with a confused and frustrated pupil population. Many otherwise intelligent students drop out.

In addition, there is no segregation between those with higher IQ and those that are struggling to learn. The groups with superior IQ obviously get bored and frustrated. To begin with they are young and do not understand how some of their classmates fail to understand what to them is only simple stuff. There are also those that have an aptitude for sports and find the facilities at school lacking and find the class work too long, boring and time consuming. This coupled with the quality of teachers and the lack of a clear policy in harnessing the different potentialities of our children leads to a high rate of school dropouts.

There is an attempt in secondary schools to try and identify students' capabilities. Students are allowed to choose about 8 subjects. Unfortunately there are hardly any criteria or justification used for the choice of the subjects. The student is inadequately guided or counselled on how to choose the subject combination. In addition, by this stage, the bulk of the would-be geniuses would have already been frustrated and dropped out of school. In order to sustain the interest of our children in the school system, there is need to do more from kindergarten, primary and secondary school up to university. We have world-class athletes, sportsmen, musicians, plumbers, painters, dramatists, academics, businesspeople, inventors, teachers, scientists, doctors and many others professions. We need to establish, in Malawi, an education and training system that challenges, and identifies these talents, gifts, passions and skills while the individual is young with a view to nurture and develop them.

For the vast majority of the people in Malawi, their lot is one that can best be described as "square peg in a round hole". People are struggling to work in fields for which they have no talent, passion or skill simply because there are no other opportunities. Herein lies the legacy of our underdevelopment and poverty. If we do not take steps to correct this aspect, our poverty will be perpetuated for a long time to come. Our graduates get all the technical and professional training in agriculture, engineering, business administration, medicine and many other fields. Unfortunately the best-trained people end up behind desks doing jobs, which any clerk can do. Our best graduates in various fields end up in administration instead of being out there creating jobs and wealth for the country.

Our best doctors are in Capital Hill doing administration work and signing cheques. This leaves the job of treating the sick to less trained and poorly equipped clinical officers and nurses. What we need are graduates in whatever field of endeavour who are prepared to go in the field and work with their hands. They should provide service to the nation with their hands. We need hands-on experts not those who serve by remote control.

Some of our best brains also end up in the Diaspora in search of greener pastures. This is largely due to poor conditions of service and a work environment that is not conducive and does not reward hard work, creativity, and diligence. There is need for a conducive work environment to be created in the country for the training and retention of our best brains. It is estimated that Liverpool in UK alone, has more Malawian doctors than all the Malawian doctors working in Malawi. These are all patriotic Malawians who have had to leave the country due to poor working conditions, political persecution, and the search for greener pastures in order to provide decent conditions of living for their families. These patriotic sons and daughters of Malawi are ready and willing to come back home to help in the nation building and economic development of the country if only an enabling environment can be established.

A word about our value system. Our value system needs to be reviewed and reinforced. We are witnessing during our time a number of people of questionable track records walking free on our streets. Some of these ought to be in jail. Unfortunately, we see them in powerful positions of influence. Instead of being condemned we see them being embraced and propelled to high positions in our society. In the developed world such people would have been ostracized. What has happened to our value system? What message are we sending to our children and grandchildren? What sort of future leaders are we breeding? This is food for thought.

Chapter Four

Believe You Can Succeed

Everyone wants to be successful. You too can be successful. Success means a lot of positive things including peace of mind, freedom to choose what you want to eat, wear, where you want to live, where to send your children to school, which car you want to drive, best medical facilities and many more wonderful things. The difference between success and failure is in the mind and in your attitude towards your setbacks, handicaps, discouragements and frustrating situations. Your thoughts and attitude determine your station in life and the level of success you will ever achieve.

Note that you can never achieve anything higher than the highest point of your dreams, imagination and goals. You are where you are because that is where you want to be! If you want your situation to change for the better, you have it in your power to do so. Indeed if you wanted your situation to be different and better, by now you should have already started the process towards changing your circumstances.

You can achieve many things in life if you truly believe that you can. If you truly desire something and if you truly believe you can achieve it, you will certainly achieve it. If you want to be successful and wealthy you will be successful and wealthy if you believe you can. Belief is critical. It follows therefore that the poor are potentially rich and successful people, but they lack the desire, drive and belief in their own potential.

Think deep and hard about the foregoing. Most of us do not take full advantage of our gifts, talents, skills, intellect, manual dexterity and other God-given assets. We also do not take advantage of the various opportunities, which are there for the taking. Poor people and rich people live in the same villages, towns and situations. Yet the rich are able to identify opportunities and become rich. The poor live in the same environment but continue to get poorer and poorer. Why?

Probably you have never thought seriously about this. Maybe you have always believed that you are poor and that it is impossible for you to make a breakthrough. Or you have always believed that what will be will be! If you want to succeed and if you believe that you can succeed and if you have strong desire to succeed, you will certainly succeed. In mini chapter 6, I encourage you, the reader, to aim high. If you aim high the level of your achievements and successes will be remarkable. Even when you experience some problems, as will usually be the case, you will still get somewhere. On the contrary, even if you aim high but you do not believe that you can do it, you will never succeed.

It has been stated by numerous authors that it is not the strongest man who wins but rather the person who has the burning desire to win and believes that s/he will win who wins. Examples abound both within Malawi and beyond regarding rich people who started out as very poor and underdogs but they thought deep and hard, decided to become wealthy, worked hard and became wealthy. Because they believed in their dreams and took necessary steps they ended up very wealthy and successful. You too can join this exclusive club. You can be successful.

For most of us, having been born in poor families, we appropriate and own the poverty as our own property. We become so entrenched in the darkness of poverty. We do not even see our way out. We do not even think and believe that it is possible to get out of our circumstances. We have no clue how to live differently. All we know is a poverty-stricken existence.

We even perfect the poverty life style. One cannot be completely wrong to believe that poor people enjoy their lifestyle and the sympathy they attract. They have all sorts of excuses regarding why it would be impossible for them to extricate themselves from their poverty. The truth of the matter is that if one so strongly desires to change one's life for the better, it is possible.

We have all seen it in our respective villages, how individuals who so deeply desired something and believed they could have it – they have worked hard at it and have become the pride of their families, communities and villages. If the desire to change one's circumstances is so strong and the individual believes s/he can have it, s/he will work so hard in a chosen project till the goal is achieved.

I recall vividly how I bought my first pair of shoes back in 1968. I was in standard four then. I recall that one of my classmates, Anusa (not real name), had a pair of shoes, which his father brought for him from the gold mines in South Africa. The pair of shoes was so beautiful. Each time he entered the classroom the pair of shoes made that characteristic knocking sound. I was all envy! I guess he also enjoyed the status that came with the possession of such a pair of shoes. From time to time he would seek permission from the class teacher to go to the toilet while the class was in progress just to attract attention of the whole class on his return. His was a special pair of shoes.

There were other boys in the class who had some other types of shoes, such as *Zonke*, and other plastic types but these were not of any consequence. It was Anusa's shoes that attracted most of the class' attention. Meanwhile I did not have any pair of shoes and was going to school bare foot. Here I was bare foot and yet my own classmate had a powerful leather pair of shoes. I made up my mind and believed that I too could have a pair of shoes similar to the one Anusa had. If you know where you want to go the how to get there everything will naturally fall in place.

Indeed where there is will there is way. I went to try and sweet-talk my father and mother into buying me the pair of shoes but my request was turned down. I must say that I was born in a poor family. It was hard enough for them to raise enough money to pay my fees. Shoes were a luxury they could ill afford. Indeed in 1969 I spent a whole academic year at home because my parents could not raise enough money to pay school fees for me and my brothers and sisters. You can therefore imagine that spending the family's meagre fiscal resources to buy a pair of shoes for me was out of question.

In fact if they had accepted to buy the pair of shoes for me my six siblings would all line up their demands for consideration. With hindsight I believe it was beneficial to me that my request was turned down. This experience taught me many lessons which have helped me in life. Since that experience I have learnt to fend for myself in many respects. I spent many sleepless nights trying to figure out how I could own such a pair of shoes. One night while lying on my reed mat, the idea came to me clearly and in no ambiguous terms.

I would go and do "*ganyu*" (piece work) everyday after school, till I would accumulate enough money to enable me buy the pair of shoes. I went to Limbe and found out the actual price of the pair of shoes. It was not a small amount by any standard. Certainly not for a standard 4 school pupil. My mind was made up. Every day after school I would go to work in our neighbour's maize gardens till late in the evenings. Mind you, one had to weed 24 maize stations (24 Metres) to get one penny (£0.01). It took me a full month working hardest every day after school to accumulate the required amount. I still have fond memories of that Saturday morning when I walked into town to buy my dream pair of shoes.

I came back home proudly swinging the paper bag containing the pair of shoes. It was the most precious possession I had. The following Monday, I too had a pair of shoes. I was no longer bare foot. What made it even more precious was that I had bought that pair of shoes with my own money – raised from my own effort, sweat and plan. I learnt a great deal from that experience. The important thing is that in spite of the seeming bottlenecks, constraints, stumbling blocks, I made up my mind that I wanted that pair of shoes. I managed to get it. Some of you can identify with this experience. What were your experiences?

Some of you were in the same class with some of our richest and most successful men and women. You can confirm that they were not the most intelligent. They were not the smartest. They were ordinary human beings. Indeed some of you have beaten them in examinations, athletics, debate, sports and even general social life. You are therefore no different from the guys who make it in life. In fact you are far more powerful than you think you are. You can achieve far greater success than imaginable if you can only believe that you can. The only difference is that successful people have, in the course of their lives, taken a decision to live successful lives. They have decided what they want to be and believed that it is do-able. On the contrary, the poor have taken a stand that it is impossible to achieve. This is the root cause of their poverty.

The poor will always come up with a long list of excuses to justify why they cannot become successful and rich. They are too old, too young, never went far with education, come from a poor family, the bank interest rates are prohibitive, their enemies have bewitched them and many more. We can all find a long list of reasons why we can never succeed. But we should not do so. The time used to draw up that list should be used more productively in terms of planning how to succeed. Actually, the wealthy and successful people do experience the same hardships but they manage to convert the problems, stumbling blocks and setbacks into opportunities. They learn to use the stumbling blocks as stepping-stones for success.

A person without a clear purpose in life will try out an impressive idea but only half-heartedly. Because in the first place s/he tries out the idea half-heartedly, when a problem strikes, s/he will fail. Indeed s/he will believe that fate is not on his/her side. Everybody experiences some frustrations, discouragement and moments of anxiety. No matter what, refuse to be discouraged. Remind yourself all the times that you will be successful. Be positive all the time. Just block negative thought from your mind. Refuse to accept defeat. When the going gets real tough, persevere. Such problems and setbacks are only meant to separate boys from men and successful people from failures.

You have what it takes to be counted amongst the successful people in Malawi. Those who do not strongly desire wealth and success will give up whenever problems appear. Have you ever watched a boxing match with millions of dollars and a world title at stake? The pundits never give up. Even when they are hurt and blood is oozing, they do not give up. The idea of giving up does not occur to them. Each of them strongly desires the world title and the millions of dollars prize money. They do not even notice that they are tired and bleeding. It is only after the last bell signalling the end of the bout that they take note of their bruises and bleeding faces. And usually it is not the strongest man who wins. It is the one who has trained hardest and the one who desires the title strongest who wins.

Once you make a breakthrough and succeeded in your chosen goal, the urge to keep on winning becomes natural. After registering the initial success you start believing in yourself. You get self confident that your goals are achievable. When I decided to write this book, there were moments of anxiety, moments when I doubted whether I would ever complete it, moments when I doubted whether at all I am a writer, moments when I said to myself – why bother. But I kept pushing on, because I knew what I wanted. I believed I could do it. In spite of the moments of doubt I kept at it. After a succession of successes you will begin to believe that the sky is the limit. Indeed, I have started drafting the second book. I am sure you will enjoy reading it as much as you have enjoyed reading this one.

After you have started achieving meaningful success, you begin to ask yourself why you did not start this process of achievement and trend much earlier. Successful people are not extra-ordinary in any way. They are only ordinary people who exert extra effort in achieving their goals. Indeed some of the rich and successful people are our own brothers, sisters, aunts, cousins, nephews, uncles, fathers, mothers, friends and acquaintances. Study their attitudes and habits, you will notice that they are ordinary people but they know what they want and where they want to go. They have a game plan so to speak.

41

No matter what happens, come rain or sunshine they have a clue about what they want to be, where they want to get and what they want to achieve. Indeed in your chosen career or business enterprise there will always be trailblazers who have already been there and have made it. I advise you to observe them carefully. Their attitude, discipline, actions and comportment will give you some idea of what is involved. Where possible seek their advice. They will be glad to show you the way.

If you are travelling from Blantyre to Lilongwe and it is really important that you get to Lilongwe, you can never return just because a bridge at Zalewa Road Block has been washed away by rain, will you? You will assess different options of getting to Lilongwe. For instance how long will it take the Ministry of Works to fix the bridge? If it will take them a week and your assignment in Lilongwe can wait for a week, you will wait till the bridge is repaired before restarting your trip. The alternative is to reroute your journey through Zomba. It is also possible to go to Lilongwe by railway. It is also possible to fly to Lilongwe. As demonstrated by this example, if you know where you are going and what you want to be, no matter what problems or stumbling blocks you face you will find a way to get there.

Most people have a kind of inferiority complex. A feeling that the task at hand is far bigger and that it cannot be accomplished. The belief that it is impossible to accomplish your plan is in itself acceptance of defeat. All of us have hidden energy, talents and skills, which only become evident when we are challenged. I recall two incidents, which have occurred in my life. These true occurrences may demonstrate how one becomes strong, courageous and fearless in the face of adversity. The first was way back in 1964 when I was a young boy. I was sleeping on a mat in my parents' bedroom. A big snake entered the house from the back door, which had been left ajar. It was a very big snake. It is nearly four decades now but through the small boy's eyes I estimate that it was more than 6 feet long and quite a big one.

The snake was entering the bedroom where I was lying down, asleep when my father saw it. The fear of that snake hurting his second born son was enough to jerk my dad into action. As the snake was only a foot from me, my father picked the nearest weapon (I believe it was a hoe) and with one heavy blow to the head he killed the offending serpent. Since that day, my dad remains my hero.

The second incident happened early in 1988. After my return from Scotland, UK where I had gone for further studies in Forestry, my first posting was at the Regional Forestry Office (South), based at Kanjedza, Limbe. Unfortunately, they had shortage of housing accommodation at Kanjedza. I was offered a house at Ndirande Forestry Office, near the Blantyre Water Board Head Office. In December 1987 I took up my post in Limbe and my house at Ndirande Forest Office. The house had just been completed but did not have burglar bars. There I was on the night of 3 March 1988, when a group of more than six thieves struck.

In one blow the attackers smashed all the windowpanes/louvers in the main bedroom. Apparently, the previous day I had planned to travel on duty to Nsanje District to supervise some urgent forestry work but had decided on the last minute to postpone till after 3rd of March. 3rd March was and still remains a public holiday. Here I was, with my wife and twin daughters, Kate and Linda, in the bedroom when the thieves struck. The feeling of being humiliated in my own house in front of my dear wife and twin daughters, whom I love, was enough to shake extraordinary strength and courage in me. Meanwhile the thieves had begun throwing stones into the bedroom in a bid to scare us away so they could collect our property.

I must confess that at first I was frightened, angry and confused. Why me, I said to myself? Meanwhile some of the stones the thieves were throwing landed on me and I felt real pain. I herded my wife and children into the corridor where they could not be hurt by the stone-throwing thugs. I returned to the bedroom to face a flurry of stones. I picked a handful of those stones, which had gathered in the bedroom and hit back with all the strength that I could muster. Meanwhile my wife kept shouting for help from the corridor where she was. It took more than 30 minutes for help to come. But I had kept the thieves at bay through the fearless action of throwing stones back at them. In fact about three of them were heard complaining about being injured as they fled. The thieves only managed to pick two pairs of trousers and a shirt, which were near the window. My wife and twin daughters are still full of praises for me up to this day - many years after the incident.

The above examples illustrate clearly that all of us have hidden reserve power, energy, talents, skills, and bravery, which only become apparent when we are challenged. Challenge yourself in business, art, music, sports, in your job and you will be surprised at the things you can do. What's more, all of us must learn to listen to the silent voice. The silent voice or intuition should be listened to all the time. Why did I not go out on field programme on that fateful 3 March 1988 as had earlier been planned? If you think and take stock of your various experiences, all of us have experienced situations when we wanted to do something but for inexplicable reasons postponed the activity. In the final analysis it proved beneficial that we had delayed doing whatever action we had planned to do.

I believe that God speaks to us through that silent voice and intuition. Please learn to listen to that silent voice all the time. Whenever you are about to do something, which is wrong, you feel a certain sense of uneasiness. If you have decided to stop drinking each time you eye that bottle of beer there is that silent voice that says, "No! Don't do it". Please take heed and listen to that silent voice. I am sure you have all heard the story of our friend Samuel (not real name).

He was invited to attend an interview for a lucrative job with the World Bank in Washington. Unfortunately the fax inviting him for the interview as well as the air ticket only arrived the day before his departure. He kept himself very busy reading some reference material and preparing for the interview such that he only left for the airport exactly one and half-hours before departure time. He took a taxi to the airport. The taxi was caught up in a huge traffic jam that he got to the airport long after the departure of his flight.

He was devastated. He was angry and frustrated that he had missed the opportunity of a lifetime. He called Washington to inform them about his predicament. Luckily for him they changed the date of his interview. Meanwhile the flight, which he missed, never made it to Washington. It caught fire in mid air. All the passengers perished. Three days later he departed for Washington. He was successful in the interview. Today he is one of the high-ranking officials at the World Bank. The turning point in our lives is when we rebel against the status quo and against ourselves. The day you say to yourself "life cannot continue like this - enough is enough." When you believe that you can do far better than your present circumstances. This is the day you have started heading in the right direction. We should learn to be dissatisfied with the status quo. There is no dignity in poverty.

Why do we get satisfied with the status quo of failure and poverty? There must be something that each and every one of us enjoys doing and something that each of us can do far better than everybody else in our neighbourhood. This is the one activity where we should consider pitching our tent. Indeed if we know where we want to go we surely will find a way to get there. If one has two goats and is satisfied with that status, there is no way that person is going to do anything about it. But if s/he is dissatisfied and wants to have ten goats, immediately his/her outlook to life and way of thinking changes. Before s/he knows it, a plan will be worked out within his/her mind to ensure that s/he can achieve the goal.

In all the villages in Malawi there are poor, relatively rich and quite rich people living side by side. Thorough study and analysis shows that the poor people do not know what they want and above all they have negative attitude to life. Rather than try to learn how their rich neighbours have managed to succeed in acquiring their status, they spend precious time and energy backbiting, denouncing and talking ill of their successful neighbours. In some cases they even go to the extent of consulting herbalists who obligingly confirm that their successful neighbours have inflicted poverty on them through witchcraft.

The successful neighbours have a positive attitude, which manifests itself through initiative, optimism, adventure, hope, faith, courage, generosity, action, good common sense and kindness. We must learn to develop a positive attitude to be wealthy and happy. Having developed the attitude to be successful, wealthy and happy, one should decide to set goals in life and develop strategies for achieving the goals. Then take necessary action.

It is important here to share with readers what my friend in Nigeria told me about setting goals. He told me, "You must always aim at the moon, because if the worse comes to the worst, at least you will end up on the roof." He went on, "if you aim at the roof, you may never leave the floor". If we set our goals high, our mind works harder in order to strategize on how to achieve the high targets set. If the goal is to have ten chickens by the end of the year the strategies to achieve this goal is certainly simpler than if the goal were to construct a mansion.

All success and achievement begins in the mind. Most people have given up on life and have stopped dreaming about success. It is a life of poverty, hopelessness and desperation. To make matters worse, there is an increase in crime rate, rot in the social fabric, downturn in the economy, unemployment and many more socio-economic ills.

There is need for everyone to resuscitate that burning desire to succeed. We need to have a country full of positive thinking individuals who have the desire to succeed. Malawians should learn to rebel from the status quo. We must learn to rebel against ourselves. The vast majority of us have been born into poverty. Once we develop a sense of dissatisfaction with our situation of poverty, hopelessness and desperation, we will start to come up with goals and strategies that can change our fortunes in life.

Most often we come across people who live other people's dreams. They see their neighbour doing something and being successful so they simply get blown by the wind and join in. In that case the person is not living his/her own dream and can only measure himself/herself against a yardstick of his/her neighbour who is the originator of the idea. We should refuse to fall into such traps. That strategy shows laziness to dream. It also shows lack of own identity and destiny. One should develop one's own dream and objectives in life, which s/he can be identified with.

Each and every person is unique in his/her own right. Each and every one of us is different. We are all inherently capable of dreaming our own unique dreams and developing our own wealth, success and happiness. Once you have dreamt and chosen your goal, clear planning, target setting and hard work should accompany it in order to successfully accomplish the desired goal. What a world of wealth and happiness would we have if all Malawians recognized and developed each and every one of their dreams?

The desire to succeed requires that one should desire to succeed. Those who think they cannot, will not. Right from the word go, one should be convinced and have that positive attitude to succeed. It is very important for all of us to set realistic goals and objectives. The successful achievement of our goals gives us that internal satisfaction and desire to continue. But once you set unrealistic goals chances are that you will fail and that failure will set in a chain reaction that convinces you that it is impossible to succeed.

Once one goal has been accomplished, we should go on and set yet another goal. Examples abound where individuals have successfully achieved their objectives but have not known what to do with their success. Rather than move on to conquer other goals it has led to their downfall. The achievement of one goal should therefore be a stepping-stone for the achievement of the next goal. This may require that one should have a ready shopping list of immediate, medium and long-term goals so that achievement of one goal should immediately lead onto strategic planning towards achievement of the next goal. It sounds difficult at first, but once you get started it will even surprise you how easy this whole subject matter is. It becomes second nature. Supposing, due to transport problems one is experiencing when going to the market, to the garden, to church, to visit relatives and attendance at many other social engagements, one set out a goal of buying a brand new bicycle by the end of 2004. Mind you this is in a village. While this may not be the most powerful dream/goal for some working class citizen in Blantyre, Lilongwe, Zomba or Mzuzu this is a perfectly realistic goal for village folk.

Once you set a goal, your mind gets to work and explores all possible avenues of achieving the set goal. A whole range of options and opportunities will be open for this person to think about in order for his/her dream to be accomplished. These will be opportunities, which have always been around, but s/he had never thought about them seriously. Our man/woman could look at various options ranging from growing potatoes, peas, sugar canes, bananas, beans, rearing local chicken or engaging in buying and selling of a range of products or other options available to him/her.

Considering the unique situation in the village, the investment options will be prioritized in terms of their financial capital requirements and practicability. All s/he needs to do is use resources at his/her disposal in terms of labour, land and other resources. His/her goal vividly stands as his/her motivation. In fact s/he will spend sleepless nights until a definite plan has been well articulated in his/her mind. Subsequently s/he will follow through his/her plan until the bicycle is purchased. Walking out of that shop with his/her bicycle in hand will be a culmination of his/her long dream. The amount of excitement, self-confidence, inner happiness and peace of mind, satisfaction and self worth is indescribable. Having achieved this dream one can see how easy it is to set a goal and stay the course towards its achievement.

Having achieved the initial goal, it would be easier to set subsequent and much more ambitious goals next time round such as having a beautiful house with burnt brick walls and iron sheet roofing. This person would have learnt the process of dreaming, setting goals, working hard towards attainment of the goal, achieving the goal, moving on to set another goal. This is the process that leads to success and prosperity. In this whole process there will be problems, set backs and other constraints, but if one is truly devoted to his/her dream s/he will sort out the problems, learn from them to either modify the goal or modify the strategy and continue towards the achievement of the goal or its modified derivative. The critical thing is to get started. One can achieve most things in life as long as one believes that one can do it. How much one achieves in life is a function of one's own imagination and belief. You can achieve most of your dreams if you can only be determined to do so.

Once one's imagination and belief have been set in motion towards the attainment of a specified goal there will always be temporary setbacks. These setbacks should be considered as mere detours. In fact, bad as they may appear, setbacks do help in making us grow and mature in the process of achieving our goals. I recall vividly our courtship. The first time I saw her something struck me about her. Her comportment, her smile, her mannerisms, her kindness, the way she spoke and many other positive characteristics. From that moment I counselled myself that whatever it takes she was one for me. I therefore started on that path to win her hand in marriage.

Most of you have travelled this path. I do not need to bore you with the minute details. You know what I mean. In short, it took a strong desire, planning and execution of the plan. In spite of the initial setbacks, persistence won the day. Why? I knew what I wanted. This is how we should all approach the achievement of all our dreams and goals in life be they social, economic and political. If the same degree of energy, perseverance and determination could be applied to all our national pursuits as we do as a people during courtship, Malawi could have been very proud of her sons and daughters.

Most Malawians leave their destiny to chance and the whims of other people. It is absolutely necessary that each and every individual should take ownership of his/her destiny. It is a very exciting but frightening experience. It is however a challenge we must all take up. Nobody can live your life for you. The achievement of one's set goals is a very powerful experience. After achieving one goal, that achievement should provide extra energy and impetus as you plan more goals to be achieved in your life. The continuous achievement of one's goals brings about our success, smiles on our faces, peace of mind and wealth. One needs to have a game plan - what one wants in life and how one wants to go about achieving it

It has been said that God the creator, having put each and every one of us on earth, He has a specific plan for you and me. Every human being is unique in his/her own right. This is why God gave you and me unique gifts, talents, skills, dreams and abilities. These inert characteristics are meant for specific purposes. They should guide you in choosing your calling and career paths. Having set your goal, it is very important to religiously stick to it no matter what. It must be added here that failure to achieve a goal should not be taken as failure. On the contrary you should learn powerful lessons from the failure and use such lessons as you plan to achieve higher goals in life.

Chapter Five

Take Advantage of Opportunities

There is pervasive poverty, hunger, disease, hopelessness, desperation, distrust, anger and many negative feelings in Malawi. The vast
majority of people have no food, are bare-foot, half-naked, sick and
live in poor houses. The picture is really grim. Unfortunately the
situation is getting worse. This picture can easily make you throw
your arms in the air in despair. But herein lie hope and your opportunity to make a difference. All the problems highlighted above and
many more provide a lot of opportunities for the discerning and those
who desire success and wealth.

The level of poverty, hopelessness and confusion in Malawi is
absolutely phenomenal. Indeed one gets the impression that people are
stuck with the doctrine of "blessed are the poor for they shall inherit
the Kingdom of God." It is as if people are competing for the "prestigious" status of the poorest of the poor hoping this will allow them a
higher claim for the Kingdom of God. It is as if to be wealthy and
prosperous is a sin. It is absolutely normal and everybody should
desire to be successful and prosperous. I believe it is everybody's
right to be successful. We should all aim to maximize our opportunities while we live. The millions of poor, bare-foot, hungry and frustrated people walking aimlessly on the streets of Malawi deserve better. They have a right to have a meaningful life. They should be given
a chance and opportunities to enhance their livelihoods.

In fact if you talk to some of the poor people they always have
powerful ideas and strategies. They can even point out errors being
committed by the rich in terms of resource use and other aspects. All
they need is the opportunity to be given a chance. They need to be
empowered and supported so they can achieve their dreams. Most of
them even have clues and a clear picture and dreams of what they
would do if they became wealthy.

It is also true that the vast majority of the poor have a mistaken
feeling that there are inadequate resources to go round and that there
must always be the poor and the rich. One also gets a feeling that they
believe that the only way you can enrich the poor is to take away part

of the resources from the rich. This is wrong. You cannot enrich the poor by impoverishing the rich.

Indeed the world has infinite quantities of money, wealth and other resources, which are available for anyone who demands them. If you desire the money so badly you will have your share. An example here is the resource distribution that goes on when a millionaire builds a multi-million Kwacha mansion in Nyambadwe. The millionaire will need an architect to design the mansion. The architect will obviously be paid. Then follows the time for construction. Lots of materials will be bought including bricks, cement, paint, nails, iron sheets, tiles, bath tabs, sinks, poles, window panes, plumbing materials, electrical wiring materials and many more.

A number of skilled and unskilled workers including bricklayers, electricians, plumbers, painters, watchmen and many more will be employed and paid wages and salaries during the construction period. After the construction of the mansion there will be finishing touches and landscaping. At the end of all this, the millionaire will have his multi-million Kwacha worth mansion. Yet the architect, the bricklayers, watchmen, plumbers, electricians, vendors of building materials and many more will also have shared the millions of Kwachas spent by the millionaire.

In addition, the value of property in the neighbourhood of the millionaire's mansion will go up. This is a clear example of how money is multiplied and distributed in many different ways. There is just too much money out there. You just have to position yourself to tap it onto your side. It is like a big river flowing through the world, all you need in order to irrigate your field and your pocket is go out there, fold your sleeves and dig a small canal that leads to your field! Voila!

The challenge is thrown to each and every person to be part of the global club of successful people. You have participated in this poverty and self-pity club for a long time. It has not been a worthwhile experience. Let us now try something different. Let us be adventurous. Let us now try success and wealth. We are sure to experience an extraordinarily sweet and satisfying feeling. Indeed as I write I already get the sensation and imagination of what it will feel like. Mind you I am in the same boat with you – I am not there yet! But I can see light at the end of the tunnel. Let us not be confused. Let us not have wild dreams about tapping from the abundant financial resources in the world. All of us should start from where we are. And start small.

To begin with, let us all commit ourselves to take stock of what resources, assets, skills, knowledge, liabilities, challenges and opportunities that we have and those within reach. There is a tendency to do this exercise quickly and assume we know it all. You need to find quality time and a quiet place where you can effectively carry out this analytical exercise. Refuse to see your environment through the same lenses as you have always done. There are so many things, which you take for granted. You have the right to see them now through a different eye and see how they can impact on your life. They are there but you do not seem to see them because you refuse to see them.

The above assessment and analysis should go beyond simply looking at the environment around you. You should also take stock of your internal and external assets and values. You should be honest with yourself in this assessment. Please write down your assets and liabilities, challenges, opportunities, skills, talents, gifts, interests, passions and experiences. Include your hobbies, likes and dislikes, educational qualifications, skills, attitudes, social values, strengths and weaknesses and many more. Be honest. You should also go a step further in identifying the opportunities that prevail in your neighbourhood.

At this point, try to see if there is any match between/among the challenges/opportunities and the assets, skills, talents, qualifications, interests, experiences that you have. I see you smiling now! Take this debate and analysis further and you have the answer to your grinding poverty. For instance what are the goods and services demanded in the neighbourhood for which you have comparative advantage in terms of your skills, knowledge, qualifications, and experience? As indicated above, there is hunger for food, shoes, clothes, music, films, drama, sports, housing, pots, plates, farm inputs, credit resources, books, newspapers, political parties, schools, colleges, snacks, restaurants. The list goes on. These are the opportunities where you and you alone can make a difference in people's lives.

Now you see clearer, don't you? Having identified the openings and opportunities you should also feel free to network and collaborate with others who in your opinion can help you achieve your objectives. I am sure you are following this with intense interest. Never be under any illusion, your burning desire to be wealthy and successful is the key and the torchlight that leads your way to freedom from poverty. If your desire is lukewarm your achievements will also be nothing to write home about. As highlighted above, let us all start from where we are. It is clear there are enormous opportunities within reach. The most valuable precious stones are not mined in the ground but in the minds of people. There is plenty of gold in your mind. Mine it and claim your wealth and place in the history of Malawi.

In our daily lives there are tools, equipment, paraphernalia, and regalia that we use as well as foodstuffs that we eat. All these provide opportunities for you. From birth to death if you have an eye for opportunity you will identify the opportunity for you to capitalize on. This assessment may have opened your eyes a little but if it has not, do not worry, do your own research and identify your own opportunities. Take it further to the point of action. This assessment will show you that some of the opportunities and challenges, which you identify, can be dealt with, with immediate effect. Of course some of these challenges require long-term planning.

There are so many goods and services, which are currently imported into Malawi. This is unnecessary. We are wasting our valuable foreign exchange for things we can easily produce locally. In addition we waste a lot of foreign exchange on unnecessary stuff. For instance why should we under the current economic hardships import cigarettes? Why can't the smokers smoke *chingambwe*! Why should we waste valuable foreign exchange to import wines, and vodkas, and brandy and other alcoholic drinks? Why not encourage consumption of locally made drinks such as Chibuku, Napolo, Carsberg, Malawi Gin and others. If we take the challenge to manufacture much of the imported goods and services locally then we could release vast amounts of our foreign exchange to be used for the importation of only essential goods and services which we are not able to produce locally.

Take the preservation and processing of our fruits as an example. Let us think through this and fully underscore the challenge. Thousands of tons of mangoes, oranges, bananas, pineapples and other fruits are wasted every year during the peak seasons. And the seasons are quite short. There is no reason to believe that Malawians would not like to enjoy these fruits throughout the year. Indeed our shops are full of imported fruit juices and fruits. We see how these products are patronized.

Our education institutions including the University of Malawi and all Primary and Secondary Schools teach science subjects. Here is a big challenge. We should find a way to preserve, can and bottle these fruits. It can be done. It must be done. Let us be committed to do the right things in order to develop our country. In so doing, as we provide useful service to our neighbours and our country we can be sure that money will find its way into our pockets.

Another aspect I want to tackle briefly is the question of tinned beef and fish. Most of us enjoy tinned fish and beef whenever we can afford it. Each time we buy these products, check at the bottom of the tin. To this day you will never see one labelled "Made in Malawi." We have the cattle resources in Lower Shire, Mzimba, Rumphi, Chitipa, Karonga, and many other places in Malawi. We have *chambo, usipa, matemba a Domasi* and other delicious fish in Malawi.

Let me confess that I am yet to taste fish anywhere in the world that tastes anywhere near *chambo*, *usipa* and *matemba* a Domasi. Our beef has a unique taste too. The world is waiting for these products. We have no right to deny the world the chance to taste the most delicious fish, beef, fruits and other products from Malawi. We have to take up this global challenge to produce high quality goods and sell them on the international market. Let us take advantage of the opportunities available to us and supply the unique Malawi products on the international market. In the process our pockets will bulge with dollars, pounds, yens, euros, nairas, cedis, and many more currencies.

It is sad that as a nation, all we know is to buy and consume goods and services produced elsewhere. Cars, fuel, computers, bicycles, tractors, videos, televisions, clothing, shoes, plates, pots, sewing needles, beer and many more. All these and many more are imported. We have imported these for a long time now. Some of these should and can be made locally. We need to think deep and hard about the legacy we want to bequeath to our children and grand children. They deserve better. We have not invented even a bicycle.

The people who invent and manufacture all the things we import into the country are ordinary people like you and me. Some of you have even been A* students in your academic life. What has happened to all that intelligence and bookishness? This shows that you have great potential, which you are not utilizing. The inventors spend sleepless nights working hard and thinking about people's wants and needs. While you and me are busy sleeping, drinking and thinking about petty issues, those with a keen eye for opportunity are busy doing research and development programmes in order to invent even better goods and services.

Let me end this mini-chapter by sharing with you a fascinating story I read in a book titled "Think and Grow Rich – A Black Choice" by Dennis Kimbro and Napoleon Hill. The authors tell of a series of lectures delivered by Dr. Russel Conwell in the early 1800s titled "Acres of Diamond." Dr. Conwell delivered the lectures about eight thousand (8,000) times to audiences across America. In the process he earned more than $8 million in lecture fees. Briefly, Acres of Diamond is about a farmer who settled in Africa. The farmer spent years struggling to grow crops. His land was rocky and difficult to till.

The farmer was fascinated by stories about people who searched and discovered diamonds in the countryside and became wealthy. He too wanted to be rich. He grew tired of the endless labour on the farm. He therefore sold his farm. For the rest of his life he wandered through the vast African Continent in search of diamonds. Sadly the riches eluded him. Finally, frustrated, angry and broken financially, spiritually and emotionally he threw himself into a river and drowned.

Meanwhile the man who bought his farm found a rather large and unusual stone in a stream that cut through the farm. It turned out to be a diamond of enormous value. The farmer discovered that his farm was virtually covered with diamonds. It was to become one of the world's richest diamond mines. The first farmer had unknowingly owned acres of diamonds but he sold the farm, including the diamonds for practically nothing in order to look for diamonds elsewhere. If only he had taken time to study and realize what diamonds really looked like in their rough state he could have found the riches he so badly wanted on his farm.

All of us are standing in our own acres of diamond. Wherever you are, you are surrounded by various acres of diamonds. You just need to have patience and the discerning eye in order to identify the available opportunities and take necessary steps to become wealthy and successful. Before you go running for greener pastures in far away lands be sure that your own pasture is not as green or even greener. Often while you're busy looking at other pastures, others are also busy looking at pastures. Let us carefully look around our environment and identify the opportunities available within reach before abandoning our station for greener pastures elsewhere. So, let us all take full advantage of opportunities within reach—and there are many.

Chapter Six

Aim High

When you aim high, you send a powerful message to the world that you are not satisfied with the status quo. That you are dissatisfied with poverty. That you are dissatisfied with what you have or the environment in which you live. All those who want something better look for that which they seek and indeed they do get it. It is in the human nature to seek something better. It is sad that the poor people in Malawi have lost this search for something better.

Once in a while we come across children from poor backgrounds that rebel against the status quo and indeed they make it big. In your search for success, note that you are not the first one. There are people who have already achieved that which you are searching for. These are people who have already travelled the distance you are planning to travel. They are trailblazers for you. It makes sense to seek their advice. You need not reinvent the wheel. Indeed, they will also be pleased to learn that there is someone out there who admires their achievements. They will be pleased to give you requisite advice. The advice you get from such people will be valuable. You could easily avoid some mistakes and take a shorter route to your desired goal if you take heed of their advice.

If you are involved in agricultural production and your set goal was to produce 20 bags of maize, chances are that due to bad weather, poor quality seed, inadequate fertilizer application, pest and disease infestation, post-harvest losses and a host of other problems you may end up getting 15 bags. It follows therefore that if you want to produce 20 bags, you may have to set your goal a little higher, say 25 bags. That way you will be sure to get at least 20 bags and may be a little more. In life there are so many surprises, which we should always be wary of.

If your goals are set too low you may not be able to achieve much. In addition it does not challenge your brain that much. The more you challenge your mind the higher the level of achievement. The challenge to do something to achieve a higher goal makes life exciting and enjoyable. The simpler the challenge the easier and therefore the less the "kick" you get out of it. When you know what you want and where you want to go, your mind goes to work in order to find the best way to get there.

For instance if you said to yourself "I want a Caducci navy blue suit." And if this desire for the Caducci navy blue suit is so strong, your mind will go to work. Within a short time your mind will present to you a detailed plan regarding what you need to do to get resources in order to buy your suit. The process as described above is the same irrespective of whether the goal in question is small or big. Now, if the process is the same, it does not make sense why we should be under utilizing our potential by setting simple goals. Why should you settle for a smaller goal when you can use the same process for a much bigger goal?

Nobody ever stumbles into success without a goal. A life without a dream or goal is meaningless. You should learn to set goals in order to get things done. Without goals you can get nothing happening in your life. Without goals individuals wander through life but do not get anywhere. You can only get somewhere if you know where you want to go and deliberately decide to get there and how to get there.

It is one thing to know where you want to go and yet a completely different thing to want to get there. You must have a goal in life. The kind of goal you have in life defines the type of life you lead. Your accomplishments, income, bank balance, lifestyle, personality, type of friends and many aspects of your life will be influenced by the nature of your goals. Setting goals for yourself is very important. If your goals are vivid and accurately defined, you will face the future with anticipation and hope. If you have no vision, no dream and no goal to look forward to, you face the future with apprehension and anxiety because you have no idea what to expect.

In your dreams, aim as high as you can. Do not limit the targets of your dreams. If your dreams are small, you will not challenge your imaginative and perceptive faculties and as a result your achievements will proportionately be small and nothing to write home about. On the other hand if you aim high even if you achieve half of your dream it will be significant and worth talking about. In setting your goal, try to be as specific as possible. A goal like "I want to be rich" is not good enough. Go further to define what exactly you mean by being rich. Do you want to have cattle? How many? Are these for production of beef or milk? Do you want to have cars? How many, and what type of cars? Do you want a Nissan, Toyota, Jaguar, BMW or Mercedes

Benz? Do you want to have a lot of property? What type and in what quantities? Do you want to have a lot of money? How much? If you define your goals or purpose in definite and measurable terms, it becomes easier to draw up plans and strategies towards their achievement.

It is easier to assess as to whether or not you are succeeding in achieving your goals if you define your goals more precisely. In other words if you know what you want and you want it so badly, you will certainly find a way of getting it. Remember there is nothing for nothing! No free lunch. After defining your goal you should be prepared to strategize on what services you are going to provide in order to actualize your dream. If a man badly wants the woman of his dream, nothing will stop him. He will do whatever is required in order to win the hand of that lady.

Unfortunately after achieving that goal most of us sit back and celebrate our conquest forgetting that there are more dreams and more goals to be accomplished in life. We get satisfied with our success that we want to sit and celebrate our success. Yes by all means we should take time to celebrate our achievements but let us not waste too much time celebrating our small successes. There are far greater challenges to achieve in life. We must always remember that life is full of mountains and valleys. After climbing one mountain, you cannot sit back and celebrate this success forever. You must plan how to scale higher mountain peaks.

The experience of achieving one goal should be helpful in the conquering of the next set of mountains. It is not right to retire after one success. If you set your goals in short, medium and long-term the momentum of having achieved the short-term goal propels you towards the achievement of the next set of goals. The strong and sweet feeling of having succeeded in the first set of your set goal should add more energy and impetus to your efforts towards the achievement of the next goal. But also learn to bite manageable mouthfuls, which you can easily chew.

As has been highlighted in numerous sections above, even with well-defined goals and well-planned strategies there will always be setbacks. Life is full of problems and nobody is exempt from this natural phenomenon. Be prepared all the time to face setbacks, problems and stumbling blocks. Always aim high.

A word to parents, teachers and spouses. What is it that you say or do to these men and women that has such negative impact on them? When they are young, these men and women have unlimited dreams, hope, expectations, beliefs, ideas, innovations, faith, courage, creativity, plans and many positive aspects. They had powerful dreams and visions about their lives. As young men and women they saw the sky as the limit. After they have gone through your hands they have lost all the dreams, energy, directions, expectations, hopes, creativity, and imagination. Indeed most of them are simply walking corpses now waiting to be buried. As young men they had burning ambitions and passions about a volume of possibilities. As they grow up, parents, teachers and spouses seem to continuously tell them what a horrible place the world is. and that nothing is possible!

Parents, teachers and spouses you are responsible. These young men and women are fed with negative paradigms of how it is impossible to achieve much due to one reason or another. These men and women who were hopeful and full of life and expectation during their childhood and teens become lifeless in their twenties and thirties and beyond. Sadly, the negative attitude is passed on from generation to generation. I believe time has come to break this vicious cycle!

All those people who achieve spectacular results aim high and have an inquisitive mind. They seek to find answers to questions. They constantly ask questions – how, why? They are not satisfied with the status quo. They are not impressed with such answers like "it has always been like this." We as Malawians have so far been satisfied with the inventions of other people. We have not contributed much to humanity. We have not even invented a sewing needle. We have not sought to challenge our imaginative and perceptive faculties. In our respective work, hobbies, and other spheres of life let us aim to change things for the better. The tools we use, the equipment we utilize, the methods we use to preserve food and other valuables, the manner in which we conduct our business all these are areas we should try and find ways to improve. Our work environment, our lives, our situation should get better.

Should Malawi remain a consumer of technological breakthroughs from far away places? The US is now conducting research on the future car that will be fuelled by hydrogen. We in Malawi have not even invented a bicycle spoke. If we look around us there are so many opportunities for our imaginative and perceptive faculties to work on.

The traditional tools and equipment we use for agricultural production in the country are the same old ones our ancestors used many centuries ago. We have a duty to improve our environment and bequeath an improved technological base to our children and grandchildren.

Our oranges in Malawi are full of seed. I believe our breeders and researchers can breed oranges with less seeds. I am sure consumers will enjoy such oranges. Our mangoes are probably the sweetest I have ever seen. But the size of our mangoes is slightly small. Our breeders can make crosses to come up with mangoes, which are as sweet, and yield a larger size. These and many more ideas should occupy the minds of our researchers and various business people. Answers to such questions would provide goods and services to Malawians and other consumers outside Malawi. It is a shame that we are doing very little in this regard. We are comfortable sitting idle and enjoying the discoveries and inventions of other people in far away places. Let us exercise our imaginative and perceptive facilities for the benefit of mother Malawi.

As you aim high in your lives you should be realistic in setting your targets. Do not be unrealistic in setting your targets. If you target buying a supersonic jet for your personal use, for instance, this could be unrealistic. Nobody can tell you how much you should dream. Nobody will tell you what targets you should set for yourself. You are the best judge in this regard. But where possible try to break down your larger dreams and goals into short, medium and long-term dimensions. This breaking of the goals makes them look reasonable and attainable.

The attainment of one set goal provides added impetus for the achievement of the next ones. For most of us, having set a short term goal say to buy a bicycle, once this is attained we tend to celebrate too much and forget that life is not just about riding bicycles. We even forget that life continues. Immediately after achieving one goal we should quickly move into setting our next goal before the excitement dies down.

Chapter Seven

Some Selected Principles of Financial Success

Success and wealth come to those people who spend time and effort planning and looking for success and wealth, people who are ready and prepared to meet the challenges and discipline involved. If you fail to plan, you should know that you are planning to fail. There is a price to pay if one desires to be wealthy and successful. If your goal is to be successful and prosperous it is important to study and emulate the lives of prosperous people. Advice on how to achieve financial success can only be sought from wealthy people – not the poor.

There are so many stories we hear about poverty-stricken and bare foot herbalists who prescribe herbs and medicines for people to become rich. One does not know whether or not to believe these stories. But if these herbalists and medicine men know the magic formula for wealth why should they go round in tattered clothes and bare feet? Why don't they use their formula to become wealthy and prosperous themselves? Don't they want to enjoy affluence and good living? Why?

A summary of selected principles on financial success is given below. These principles have been endorsed by some of the wealthiest tycoons in the world. I have read a few books regarding the topic of success and wealth. In almost all these books there is agreement on these basic principles. In this mini-chapter I will share with you some of the principles through which some people have acquired physical wealth and financial success. I urge you to try these principles. If they have helped others in their search for wealth and financial success, they should be able to help you as well.

1)   Earn Your Money

For any money you get, you should provide services equivalent to the amount you receive. There is nothing for nothing. If you receive money through deceitful means that money does not belong to you. Indeed you should be ashamed to take possession of money, which you have not sweated for. You will never have peace of mind if you take possession of money, which does not belong to you.

God gave you gifts, talents, skills, energy and other assets. Use them to earn money for yourself. The harder you work in using your God given talents and assets to provide much-needed goods and services in your neighbourhood/community the more your earnings will be. It is not enough to wish. We all wish we had volumes of money to enable us afford some of the things which are currently out of reach. Beyond wishing we should take steps to plan, work hard in order to earn the money we want.

2) Pay Yourself First

The income you get through your various jobs and businesses is used in many different ways. The money is used to buy clothes, paying school fees, rent, medical bills, water, electricity, telephone, helping your parents and many other important things in life. In other words most of us live a hand to mouth existence. The money you earn is not adequate to cover all your needs and wants. Month end is a sad period as you have to pay all your bills, your creditors are waiting to be paid, school fees has to be paid, your dependants are waiting for pocket money and many more things need to be done.

Every month you and I hope that one day our salaries will be enough to meet our growing lists of wants and needs. As we grow older our financial obligations also grow in order to meet the cost of educating our children in secondary schools and university as well as taking care of our aged parents.

But there is no evidence whatsoever to prove that anyone ever grew prosperous with a salary. If your goal is to be wealthy then look elsewhere – not a salary. If you do not effectively plan your exit from the vicious cycle of poverty you will remain in there till your retirement day.

The sad thing is that all the money you earn ends up buying stuff and paying bills. Yet you the one who sweat in the hot sun every day and in unfriendly work environments do not get your fair share. From whatever earnings you make, learn to set aside something for yourself. Pay yourself first before you start the rounds of payment of bills and purchases. Pay yourself at least 10% of your net earnings. Depending on your level of net earnings and commitments you can even push your pay upwards to 20% of your net income. This amount is yours to keep. It is your payment for the labour, energy and effort you put in your work. Save it in a safe savings account for it to grow. All for you.

You must decide to start paying yourself now! It is not an easy decision to make but it must be made. The often-made excuse is "how can I save when my income is not even enough to meet my expenses?" Where there is a will there is a way. The truth is that no matter how much your income is, if you do not plan your expenditure, you will still find that before the next pay period you are already broke. All of us have infinite needs and wants but our means are limited. You should discipline yourself and commit yourself to save at least 10% of your net earnings. Soon you will get used to an expenditure pattern that fits within the remaining 90% of your net income.

Those who have tried this plan have success stories to tell. They will tell you that it makes a lot of difference in one's life. From the moment you take this decision you cease to live a hand to mouth existence. The first thing that happens if you follow this principle is that it enhances your self-confidence and self esteem. Supposing that your monthly net earnings are about K1,000. I know that, you the reader, your monthly net income is by far more than this figure. But for argument's sake let us take K1,000. If you save 10% (K100) every month, your annual savings will be K1,200. This is not a simple feat by any standard for somebody earning K1,000 a month as net income. If you put this amount in a savings account, the total balance in your account will be K1,200 plus interest at the current interest rate.

For argument's sake if we assume the interest rate is 20% then you will have K1440 in your account at the end of the year. But we all know the interest rate in Malawi is by far more than this. You will therefore join an exclusive elite club of a handful of people who have learnt to live within their means and can boast of some savings in a bank account. Mind you, there are not many Malawians who have balances in their savings accounts! The vast majority live a hand to mouth existence and have to borrow to cover shortfalls from time to time. The feeling of watching your money grow is so powerful and fulfilling. It is beyond description. It is like walking on the moon, I guess – as I have never been to the moon!

When you start saving at least 10% of your income, the remaining 90% should be used to cover those expenses including buying clothes, paying school fees, rent, medical bills, water bills, electricity bills, telephone bills, paying off your debts, helping your parents and many other important things. Earmark 10% of this amount for debt repayments. This will give you additional peace of mind to know that no creditors are following you. In addition 10% should also be set aside for charity and other causes. If you are a Christian this amount should be used to pay your tithe and contribution towards success of your church activities.

3) Control Your Expenditure

After you have saved at least 10% of your net income, the remaining 90% will not be adequate to cover all your wants and needs. It is almost impossible to satisfy all your wants and needs. In fact as your level of income and influence grows the list of what we may regard as necessary expenditures grows. Herein lies the need to prioritize, plan and budget your expenditure. You should establish a priority list of essential items on which you want to spend your money on. Cross out those that are not essential.

The purpose of a budget is to help you screen out unnecessary expenditures and ensure that only essential items are taken care of. Your budget will certainly include things like education for your children, house rent, food, clothes, medical care, transport, water bills, electricity bills, telephone bills, debt repayment, miscellaneous expenses and of course a bit of leisure. It is important to include a bit of leisure for it is said "all work and no play makes Jack a dull boy" It is important to make time to go out and relax and enjoy yourself. But do not overdo it!

Note that you must always include miscellaneous expenses in your budget. These are the inescapable expenses but those you can never predict. These come about from time to time, especially within the framework of our culture in Malawi. With our extended family system there are always demands placed on you, which come from time to time and demands that you help out. There will always be funerals, weddings, and school fees for nephews, aunts, cousins, uncles, and support for parents and grandparents. Some of these relatives will visit you in your house in the city to solicit your help. You should never abandon your cultural obligations. You should always feel duty bound to provide some help, where you can.

But remember, in the process of helping others, you should never over-stretch yourself. Do not inherit the burden that does not belong to you. It is important to point out here that in meeting your social and cultural obligations you should not be forced to draw down on that 10% which you paid yourself which should be growing in a savings account somewhere.

4)   Invest, Invest, Invest

As has been described above, the feeling of seeing your bank balance grow is quite a powerful sensation. The savings in your bank account could be wisely invested and earn you substantial regular income. If you invest strategically, your income and profits will be substantial. Before you make any investment, it is advisable that you should seek expert counsel, advice and guidance. If you intend to invest in a fishing enterprise, please consult the fisheries experts. If you intend to invest in a firewood and charcoal business by all means consult the forestry experts. If you want to invest into buying and selling, you will be safe to seek advice from a Marketing Expert. Your bank manager should also be consulted. He is in the money sector and can provide you with valuable advice.

Having disciplined yourself to save 10% of your net income, it would be foolhardy to allow yourself to be duped into wasteful and unprofitable investments by tricksters. Whatever investment you decide to go into, make it a point to ensure that your capital is safe even in case of adversity. There are many investment opportunities in Malawi. Identify the one that is for you. Be prepared to seek advice from experts. There are many experts in the country who can help.

While we are on this sub-topic, let us reflect a little. Why is it that all the major businesses in Malawi are owned by foreign individuals and companies? We have a lot of brothers and sisters out there in all major world capitals who have a lot of money. Why do they choose not to invest in Malawi? They are comfortable sending a few dollars once in a while to their parents and relatives, but shun away from significant investments. Some of them are comfortable purchasing property and expensive cars abroad. While some of them may not be too sure about the prevailing opportunities in the country there are many who find the socio-economic and political environment not conducive for investment in mother Malawi. But if the socio-economic and political environment is not conducive, how come the foreign investors find it conducive to invest?

There is a challenge here for our policy makers and political masters to ensure that they create an enabling environment for the rich

Malawians both within and in Diaspora to invest in the country. It may also be worthwhile for the Malawi Chamber of Commerce, MIPA, Export Promotion Council and other similar bodies to make deliberate effort to sensitise the rich Malawians locally and abroad to invest in the country. There is no doubt that such an aggressive pro-investment strategy can lead to more business activities, more jobs, wealth creation, export trade, import substitution and more foreign exchange earnings.

5)   Live in Your House and Grow Your Own Food

As the month draws to a close, there is a common feeling that runs through the mind of all of us who live in rented houses. If you are lucky that your employer pays house rent for you, this reduces the level of your tension. But the majority of us have to pay our own rentals. If you are self-employed and your business has not been good in the month you are unable to pay your rental. In this case you go through painful feeling of having to beg your landlord to give you a few more days. If you have your own house, your financial obligations are reduced considerably.

You can build or buy a house of your choice. I have seen with my own eyes how some general workers I worked with a couple of years ago built modest houses for themselves. They bought a piece of land adjacent to each other on the outskirts of the city, and within reasonable walking distance to work place. First of all they built makeshift structures of wood and plastic roofing. With time I observed that they had moulded bricks. Within a period of two years they had brick wall structures with windowpanes, but the roofing was still plastic sheet.

The following year I noticed that part of the roofing was now of corrugated iron sheets. The following year they completed the roofing. If those labourers could do it, why can't other labourers do the same? Better paid clerical staff, professional staff, and management staff, chief executives, self-employed people can also do it. I challenge everyone to follow the example of these general workers who had a vision. They were determined, worked hard, persevered and finally achieved their desired goal. Learn a lesson from them.

Apart from the happiness and self-confidence that comes with owning a home, the amount of money you have always used to pay rent, will now become available for other uses. It will no longer go to the landlord. As you approach retirement, your mind will be at ease if you have your own house. I have known many senior civil servants who retired without a home. They only started constructing houses when the terminal benefits were paid to them. Pension money is not for house construction. Almost all of them never managed to complete the houses with the pension money. Some of them ended up selling the plots and the half completed structures at give away prices.

It is also advisable, to grow your own food. Grow your own maize, vegetables, okra, *denje*, cabbages, tomatoes and *nkhwani*. Indeed, home-grown food tastes much better than what you buy from the market. Where one lives in the city this may be a bit difficult. But consider to rent a plot just outside the city where you can grow your crops. You can spend your weekends supervising workers on your small farm. Growing your own crops will reduce your budgetary requirements for food but will also ensure high quality nutrition for the family.

6) *Ensure a Future Income*

As a young man/woman, ensure your future income through education and training. Make sure that you are well trained and skilled for your future career. That way you will effectively be able to provide for yourself and your family. As you grow older, you should always make arrangements to ensure that in your old age there will still be an income to provide for your needs and wants. There are many ways you can do this. You can invest in physical assets like houses and business premises. These can provide you with rentals even during your old age. You can adequately educate your children. This is also some insurance for your old age. Your children will feel obliged to return the favour.

You may decide to subscribe to an insurance policy where you deposit a prescribed sum during your working life. During your retirement, when the insurance policy matures you can get your dues. The money can be put in a bank account where it can generate interest on regular basis. A number of employers also provide some pension fund. When you retire they give you a gratuity and thereafter on monthly basis they give you a pension to keep you going.

7) *Enhance Your Ability to Earn*

If you are to achieve financial success the first step is to have a strong and definite desire for wealth. The desire should be strong and definite. Definite is the qualifying word. If you say you want to be rich - this is not definite. You need to define your desire more precisely. Do you want K4 million or K10 million or K20 million? Be precise and definite about what you want. And please write down your goal. From time to time preferably twice daily read your definite goal to make sure it is well imprinted in your mind. In addition, study the way successful people conduct themselves in business or at the work place. Try to learn some tricks from them and emulate their example. Consult successful people in your line of work and/or business. Exchange views and ideas with powerful people. It will help you.

Get trained in one trade or the other. It is easier for you to get a job if you are a qualified applicant than an unskilled labourer. I therefore encourage each and every Malawian to train in one trade or the other. Train as carpenters, bricklayers, welders, mechanics, tailors, blacksmiths, nurses, computer operators, drivers, fishermen, agriculturists, engineers, lecturers, teachers, and a host of other professions. This increases your ability to earn than if you are unskilled.

Technology is evolving from time to time. Do not be left behind. Teach yourself how to use computers, and other modern technology appliances. If you have a Junior Certificate and you want a better-paid job, go back to school and get an MSCE. Nowadays there are a lot of evening classes available in many parts of the country. Enrol in one of them. Most high paying jobs require candidates who are computer literate. If you want a high paying job, get a computer literacy course. If you are a grade 3 mechanic, upgrade yourself to get grade 2 and grade 1 and City and Guilds. If you have a Bachelors Degree, upgrade yourself to get a Masters Degree and PhD. Continuously upgrade yourself. If you are into buying and selling, find cheaper sources of your merchandise, which will improve your profit margin.

8)   Help the Poor

It is more blessed to give than to receive. I learnt this lesson from my parents a long time ago when I was a little boy. No matter how little you have, there are others who are in far greater need than yourself. Learn to be compassionate and share the little you have with those who are in dire need. Donate to charitable causes including support for orphans, widows, the aged, the sick and other people who are less fortunate than you.

If you are a Christian, the Bible teaches us to tithe – to give 10% of our earnings to support God's work. And there is a promise in that verse in Malachi that says God will open the heavens and you will not even have enough storage space for the abundant blessings that will rain on you. As we all know, our Heavenly Father always fulfils His Promises. I have no doubt He will shower you with abundant blessings if you give to charity and also if you tithe. Try Him! Something I have learnt with time is that God does not give you more if you hold on tightly to the little that you have. Let go the little that you have to good cause you will be surprised how much more God will give you. Find a good cause, which you can identify with. Give cheerfully. God will bless you and give you abundant physical and financial blessings.

Just as you cannot reap without sowing, God requires of you to give cheerfully to the sick, the orphans, the poor and the homeless. That is how you sow to ensure an abundant harvest from your Heavenly Father. If you want to enjoy wealth, prosperity and have peace of mind, begin today by donating cheerfully to a worthy cause. Pray unceasingly. Ask for God's guidance in all your endeavours as you work towards achieving your goals and purpose in life. Be a good steward of whatever little you have. Through donating to good cause, you bring smiles to otherwise miserable people. God richly blesses those who donate to the poor and downtrodden. Learn to use the little you have to make what you want it to be by donating to good cause. God bless you all.

Chapter Eight

Agriculture

Agriculture is the backbone of the Malawi economy. The country has one of the most fertile agricultural soils in Africa. Agriculture contributes about 40% of Gross Domestic Product (GDP). The sector also accounts for about 85% of the country's export earnings. Maize is the main food crop and grown on about 95% of the cultivated area in Malawi. Other economically important crops include tea, cotton, sugarcane, cashew nuts, macadamia nuts, tung, groundnuts, rice, coffee, cassava, beans and pulses. Tobacco is by far the most dominant export earner, accounting for more than 70 percent of agricultural exports. The other main cash crops are tea, which makes up 7.5 percent, sugar at 7.4 percent, coffee peaking at 4.1 percent and cotton at 0.5 percent.

The country's export earnings are derived from tobacco (59%), tea (19%), groundnuts (2%) and other crops (12%). More than 80% of the Malawi population live in rural areas and are engaged in agricultural production. Over the past decade more than 20% of the country's food requirements have had to be imported. In the last two years alone drought and floods have compounded the situation thereby making the country dependent on donor support to cover food deficit. With more than 80% of our population engaged in agriculture we are still unable to be food self-sufficient.

In America and other developed economies only 10% of the population live on farms and produce more than enough food to feed the entire nation with huge surpluses supplied to feed the hungry people in the developing world including Malawi. Certainly there is something wrong with our agriculture sector policies in Malawi. There are various aspects of our agricultural production that require attention ranging from appropriate technology, government support, marketing, agro-processing and export promotion.

The country's agricultural production derives from the smallholder agriculture and estate farming. Smallholder agriculture accounts for over 85 percent of production, which meets the country's demand for food staples. Some surplus from the smallholder sub-sector is also exported. The estate sub-sector however contributes 12% of total agricultural production but accounts for about 70% of all agricultural exports. It is estimated that the total land under cultivation in the smallholder agricultural sector is about 1.5 million ha. Given the growing global anti-smoking lobby Malawi may have to seriously begin to identify alternative export crops, as tobacco may gradually become unprofitable.

Malawi's economic reliance on exports of primary agricultural commodities renders it particularly vulnerable to external shocks. Being a landlocked country, high transport costs, which in some cases comprises over 30% of its total import bill, constitute a serious impediment to economic development and export trade. While Malawi relies on export of primary agricultural products, the country is a net importer of manufactured goods. Malawi imports almost all manufactured goods, farm inputs, machinery, industrial raw materials, luxury goods and many more. Paucity of skilled labour, difficulty in obtaining expatriate employment permits, and inadequate and deteriorating roads, electricity, water, and telecommunications infrastructure further hinder economic development in the country. The Government would do well to rehabilitate and improve the infrastructure in the land.

For a long time the Government of Malawi has subsidized the price of fertilizers and other farm inputs. Of late however, the donor community has advised the government to consider reducing subsidies on farm inputs among others. The argument is that it is not sustainable. The irony is that the same donor community spends billions of dollars subsiding farmers in their respective countries. While indeed it is true that the government cannot sustain the budgetary pressures of the subsidies, other options could have been explored to support poor farmers' agricultural production – particularly food production.

Today it is only farmers in the developed countries who are able to produce competitively and dump their products in the market place in developing countries at cheaper prices. Small-scale farming in developing countries is no longer profitable and viable. Smallholder farmers in the developing countries must find ways and means to survive. One means is to ensure that they explore innovative ways of minimizing production costs. What a tall order!

One area requiring attention in the agriculture sector is appropriate technology. It is clear that the same old hoe and handle are in use today as they were more than 200 years ago. The conditions and circumstances have since changed a great deal yet the technology remains the same. Back then, the population of Malawi was less than 1 million. Yet today Malawi has about 11 million people. The challenge of feeding 11 million people by hoe wielding peasant farmers is enormous. The agricultural scientists have a challenge here to invent appropriate technology that is responsive to our set of environment, social and economic conditions. In parts of Malawi farmers use ox-drawn implements to work their fields, but this technology is not widely used, as some parts of the country do not have a tradition of keeping oxen.

Adequate funding needs to be provided for research and development. This is critical in the identification of area specific technologies taking into account the variations in social, cultural and economic circumstances. Tractors have been adopted in some countries to alleviate drudgery in agricultural production. To what extent is such mechanization sustainable? Is such policy and strategy applicable to Malawi? Some research results indicate that this is not sustainable as the economic base and technical know-how of the small-scale farmers may not support this level of technology. The immediate results are however encouraging as farmers do not have to use their muscles and hoes to prepare land. Tractors provided by Government would be handy to do the job. More thinking is required to address the question of technology in our farming activities in Malawi.

Irrigation is another important area Malawi should invest in to ensure that she can maximize agricultural output. The country has five lakes and many river systems with potential for irrigation. The Shire River drains water from Lake Malawi and Lake Malombe. This important river system empties into Zambezi River. The Shire River meanders its way through almost half the length of the country and empties its load into the Zambezi. While hydropower generation schemes have been developed along the river there is need to develop sustainable irrigation systems to enhance agricultural production. Rather than relying solely on rain fed agriculture irrigated agriculture holds the key for the country's food self sufficiency as well as the development of export potential. Both small-scale and large-scale irrigation schemes should be explored.

Malawi should heavily invest in agro-processing. The country continues to export large quantities of primary agricultural products. Much of the exports are raw agricultural products, which are processed elsewhere. This sector offers some of the greatest investment opportunities for job creation and generation of food and wealth. Apart from processing raw agriculture produce for export, development of related industries such as manufacturing plants for fertilizer and pesticides, and expanding cash crop production should be considered. Take tobacco for instance, over the years the country has exported quality tobacco leaf to western markets at low prices. In turn the country has been importing cigarettes and tobacco-based insecticides and other chemicals at very exorbitant prices. You do not need a sophisticated economist to show you that this policy is wrong and perpetuates our poverty.

The balance of trade has therefore not been in our favour. It is high time the country adopted a policy of exporting more processed or semi-processed products. This policy if adopted will open up a number of agro-processing units throughout the country thereby creating much-needed jobs. In addition to creation of wealth and jobs this strategy will make rural areas more attractive thereby stemming the rural-urban migration. This would also have the advantage of consolidating the social fabric, as families would stick together as opposed to the current situation where there are many absentee spouses who go to the cities in search of remunerative employment.

Several crucial economic reforms have and continue to take place. Structural adjustment programme; liberalization of trade; withdrawal of government support to agricultural parastatal organizations, which have been instrumental in the marketing of inputs as well as farm output; globalization and many other changes. These changes pose severe challenges to the farming communities in Malawi. Farmers have to face international market competition in the globalized market. Unfortunately the playing field has not sufficiently been levelled for the poor Malawian smallholder farmer to effectively compete. While the farmers in the developed countries receive massive subsidies, the poor farmers in Malawi have had their government support withdrawn. The farmers have to buy their farm inputs at market prices. Profitability of agricultural enterprises is therefore at its all time low. What should they do?

Instead of applying inorganic fertilizers, for instance, our farmers should consider applying animal manure, compost manure and other forms of organic fertilizers. In addition instead of applying pesticides and fungicides they should explore the use of plant material such as Neem and other plants, which have fungicidal and pesticidal properties. In livestock production, smallholder farmers should consider the use of local breeds fed with locally mixed animal feed. They should learn the technology of mixing the animal feeds from locally available ingredients such as soybeans, pigeon peas, beans, *matemba*, leucaena and others.

The prevailing market challenges call for different survival strategies. Our agriculture extension agents and agriculture research should help the poor farmers come up with survival strategies. The agriculture research programme and agenda should be home grown. In addition to addressing the challenges mentioned above there should be deliberate effort to identify and breed superior quality products for which Malawi has a competitive advantage. Often we see our researchers busy doing high-tech research in line with what other researchers are doing world-wide. Time has come for our researchers to conduct more on-farm research with a view to find answers to the challenges facing our farmers in today's world. Their research should be responsive to our socio-economic concerns, problems, constraints and aspirations.

The farmers on their part need to be organized into farmer groups, clubs, women farmers groups, associations, co-operatives and other groupings, which will enable them pool their resources. In addition such groupings will also allow them to speak with one voice. Another advantage will be that banks and other financial institutions will be more willing to extend loan facilities to organized farmers than to individual poor farmers. Furthermore, farmers need to rise to the various challenges through collective strategies in order to protect themselves from the exploitative tendencies by the business people. Such groupings can be used for collective bargaining but can also serve the purpose of improving competitiveness and economies of scale. The government needs to put in place institutional framework and infrastructure that will ensure fair practices and support to farmer associations. Farmers must find creative ways to remain competitive and keep their operations profitable under the new economic order.

More and more farmers should also be encouraged to engage in export-oriented farming. There is high demand on the international market for flowers, soybeans, paprika, cashew nuts, macadamia nuts, rice, groundnuts, beans, peas, and much more. Malawian farmers have to take advantage of these economic openings. For many years the agriculture policy of the country has focused on food self-sufficiency.

As the staple food in Malawi is maize, the citizenry has been forced to grow maize even on soils that are not best suited for maize production in the name of food security. Farming is a business and farmers must learn to take decisions on the basis of economic viability.

In today's new economic order farmers should rethink their strategy towards producing agricultural crops for which they have capacity and comparative advantage. For instance, there has been a policy encouraging maize production throughout the country to promote food security. In soils that cannot support maize production, it would be advisable for the farmers to grow crops for which they have clear comparative advantage. Incomes accruing from sales of such crops can be used to meet their socio-economic obligations including school fees, medical bills, domestic needs as well as purchase of food requirements. Farmers who enjoy comparative advantage for maize production will in turn take advantage of the challenge posed by such a shift in policy. They would have to increase their productivity and production with a view to meet the increased demand for maize.

The World Trade Organization (WTO) to which Malawi is a signatory, provides international trade guidelines compelling countries to open up their markets to international trade. The WTO rules and regulations play in the hands of farmers and manufacturers in the developed countries. As farmers and manufacturers in the developed countries are heavily subsidized they are able to produce at competitive prices and are able to dump their products at the doorsteps of the developing countries cheaply. On the contrary, the poor farmers and manufacturers in the developing countries are left to their fate.

The poor are getting poorer while the rich are getting even richer. This has led to problems of closure of many farms and industries in the developing countries. Malawi has not been spared. Many industries have been closed. Farmers and manufacturing industries in developing countries simply cannot make profits in the face of such stiff competition. The Government needs to find innovative ways of supporting and protecting its farming communities and manufacturing industries without breaking the WTO rules and regulations. They should explore the possibility of exacting sizeable import duty for imported goods to enable the country to collect revenues as well as increase local production. Initiatives should also be afoot to promote consumption of locally produced goods and services.

A special fund could be established in which part of the customs duty could be deposited for purposes of supporting local farmers and manufacturers. The government and business gurus in the country should also put their heads together to come up with appropriate incentive systems for manufacturers and farmers to ensure that they remain in business. This will enable local businesses and farming enterprises continue to generate wealth as well as create jobs for the school leavers and millions of unskilled labour force in the country.

Globalization is here to stay. Farmers in Malawi and other parts of the developing world have to adapt to the global challenges or face extinction. The changes that have been brought about by globalization as described above have left a trail of hardships in the farming communities. Farmers are faced with problems ranging from high input prices, low output prices and no organized market outlets. This is making agricultural enterprise risky and less viable. These are realities, which every farmer has to face. Viewed from a negative perspective, farmers become very frustrated and demoralized. However viewed from a positive perspective, there are opportunities which can be tapped.

This frustration is manifested in a variety of ways including excessive beer drinking, polygamy, rural-urban migration and less effort being put in agricultural production. Unfortunately those who venture into the cities in search of off-farm remunerative employment are faced with yet other shocks such as downsizing, unemployment, crime, homelessness, and lack of social support systems.

Structural adjustment programmes have led to downsizing of many industries leading to massive retrenchments. Globalization has brought about a number of problems that can be converted to opportunities if one has a keen eye for opportunity. Donors have steadily reduced their funding during the 1990s for rural development, especially roads and other transportation networks, and agricultural research and extension systems. Smallholder farmers have to adapt through improvement of their skills, develop new strategies, plan and implement new activities and become efficient and effective players in the global economic arena. The vacuum created by withdrawal of government and parastatal organizations from marketing and distribution of farm inputs and agricultural produce has to be filled by farmer groups, community based organizations (CBOs), Non Governmental Organizations (NGOs), the elite and rich people in our country.

The emergence of a cadre of individual businesspeople and businesses involved in input distribution and marketing of agricultural produce is a welcome development and should be encouraged. However, the private companies and traders that have emerged as a result of the closure of state commodity boards are in many respects too small and too weak to provide the services and infrastructure needed to deal with the situation. Their capacity and level of operations does not compare with what prevailed when the government parastatal bodies were in operation. Due to the supply-demand situation prevailing during time of harvest, farm gate prices are quite low. This does not reward the farming communities adequately for their labour, time, inputs and management cost.

Unfortunately, the farmers are very vulnerable at this time as their requirements for cash are very high. The farmer will have spent the entire farming season working and is ready to get financial reward for his/her labour. The farmer therefore needs cash very urgently at this time to pay school fees and other social-economic obligations. The buyers therefore take advantage of the farmers' predicament and pay low prices. Here too there are lots of opportunities for those with a `discerning eye.

Chapter Nine

Eco-Tourism

Malawi has a huge comparative advantage for eco-tourism. Malawi is one of the most beautiful countries on earth. It has a picturesque and breathtaking landscape. The landscape ranges from the Rift Valley floor along the Shire Valley and Lake Malawi at about 500 meters above sea level through the Shire Highlands to the mountainous areas up to the peak of Mount Mulanje. The highest peak on Mulanje Mountain is about 3,000 meters above sea level. Generally the people in Malawi are very hospitable, kind, generous, peace loving, God-fearing and welcoming. This is why Malawi is called the "Warm Heart of Africa".

The country has abundant fresh water Lakes - Lake Malawi, Lake Malombe, Lake Chilwa, Lake Chiuta, and Lake Kazuni. The Shire River drains Lake Malawi and Lake Malombe and meanders its way through the countryside and discharges is water load into Zambezi River. Anyone who has visited the country is sure to return. The principal tourist attraction in Malawi is Lake Malawi, which is set among rolling hills covered in tropical vegetation. Resort areas around Lake Malawi include Mangochi, Salima, Nkhata Bay, Chilumba, Karonga. Bird life at Lake Malawi is wonderful. The opportunities for bird watching in Malawi are boasted as one of the best in South Eastern Africa. The Lake has one of the highest diversities of fresh water fish in the world. Fishing for salmon, bream, black bass and tiger fish is a popular pass time.

Chambo, utaka, usipa, ntchira, milamba and all other sweet tasting fresh-water fish in Malawi add value to the tourist experience in Malawi. Lake Malawi has over 750 species of unique fish, which are endemic to Malawi. In addition the country has game reserves and national parks where you have wonderful wild life viewing experiences. These are Nyika, Lengwe, Liwonde and Vwaza Marsh. In addition there are numerous protected forests, which add an aesthetic value to the landscape. Around Cape Maclear there are excellent snorkelling and diving spots.

Some of the interesting places that should be targeted for marketing to the tourists worldwide include national parks and wildlife reserves;

Forest Reserves, Mulanje Mountain; Kapichira and Nkula Water Falls and their associated bird life; Lakeside resorts including Mangochi, Chilumba, Karonga, Nkhata Bay, Salima, Cape Maclear, and Likoma and Chizumulu Islands. Bird life such as African fish eagles, Palm nut vultures and fishing owls are prolific among the flood plains and reed swamps. Malawi is also home to herds of elephant, hippo, waterbuck, reedbuck, zebra and sable antelope. It should also be noted that Malawi has one of the largest number of orchid species in Africa. Zomba Mountain is one of the best places for orchids and other native flora. A variety of locally produced quality handicrafts can be found in the tourist centres including Mangochi, Salima, Karonga, Nkhata Bay, Blantyre and other places. Most of these are made from wood, clay, soapstone, beads, raffia and reeds, and are well priced for tourists.

With the smiling people, the picturesque landscape and the wonderful game reserves, national parks, forest reserves, mountains and beautiful semi-tropical climate, tourism ought to be a multi-billion dollar industry. But it is not. What is the problem? First and foremost is the problem of political will. For inexplicable reasons, there is apparently no political will to develop this industry. For the last three decades under the first republic, there were funny dress codes that kept the tourists out of Malawi. Tourists were not allowed to wear long hair, they were not allowed to wear bell-bottom trousers, and women were not allowed to wear mini skirts or trousers and many restrictive rules and regulations. This kept the tourist away leading to capital flight.

In addition, the country was largely a police state where one could be picked and locked in detention for speaking against the establishment. Many tourists were detained for days and deported back to their countries of origin. Such unfriendly dress codes and cases of deportations for petty offences received massive negative publicity. As a result the country lost out from being a priority tourist destination. Although we now have democracy, a number of factors still militate against the flow of tourists into Malawi.

Malawi boasts of a rich and diverse culture, ethnic groups, dialects and various foodstuffs, which can be profiled for tourist attraction and consumption. There are also many traditional dances in Malawi, which are unique. Some of these include Gule Wamkulu, Manganje, Mwinoghe, Mganda, Ndolo, Beni, Chioda, Chimtali, Tchopa, Malipenga, just to mention a few. Even amongst Malawians, depending on where one comes from one may not have had an opportunity to see all the traditional dances. For the tourists, it would be a real treat to sample some of these. To support a tourist industry there is need for the Government to invest in upgrading the infrastructure. There is also the need to promote internal tourism. Statistics in the neighbouring countries show that the largest tourist market is the indigenous people. There is need to deliberately target that market.

The infrastructure in the country is not only inadequate but also of poor quality and the standards continue to decline. The country has one of the lowest per capita telephone, fax and email systems. The road network is in a sorry state. There are only about 10 hotels of international standard with less than 3,000 beds among them. The in-country transport system is also deplorable. These and many other statistics relating to the infrastructure in the country do not provide the needed support for a sustainable tourism industry. The role of Government is to establish an enabling environment for the private sector to play its role in providing the needed services in the industry. In addition the government needs to build and rehabilitate the requisite infrastructure. The Government is therefore failing the country in this regard.

Recently a female tourist was killed in Cape Maclear, in Mangochi. A few years ago a tourist was robbed in Mzuzu. Although the country is relatively very peaceful and hospitable such statistics do not help to attract more tourists. While there are few cases of murder, mugging and robbery against tourists the Government needs to take steps to completely eliminate any danger to the prospective tourist. The few cases that occur are reported to nearest Police Stations. The Police do not seem to have a long-term strategy for dealing with such cases.

One would have expected the major tourist areas of the country to have well trained and well equipped police officers. This is not the case. Where the police officers have been posted they are poorly equipped. In many cases if one calls the police for help after being attacked or robbed, it is common for the police to request the victim to provide the needed transport. How on earth does the police expect the victim of a robbery or violent crime to provide transport and logistics to the police whose job, in the first place, is to protect lives and property!

The private sector participation and involvement in the tourist industry requires massive capital injection in order to provide high quality hotels, campsites, trails, and yachts on the lakes, boats, and other recreational facilities. The financial institutions in Malawi charge interest rates, which are prohibitive. Such high interest rates make our financial institutions ideal for short-term borrowing only. With interest rates of more than 40% it is difficult to envisage how one can borrow for long-term investment ventures such as development of tourist infrastructure. As will be discussed in the ensuing mini chapter, the country should explore alternative ways for making credit facilities available for development purposes. This is a critical aspect and one of the basic prerequisites for development. Where there is a will, there is a way.

At present there are several constraints that hinder the development of tourism. Some of these constraints include: lack of political will; lack of investment in international-standard accommodation and tourism facilities; inadequate and poor infrastructure which limit access to most tourist attraction areas in the country; lack of specific incentives for private sector investment; and inadequate marketing campaigns in Malawi's major markets. These issues, problems and constraints have to be addressed.

Chapter Ten

Micro Credit

There are a lot of opportunities in Malawi for the discerning Malawian. Indeed many Malawians have brilliant investment ideas aimed at taking advantage of the unlimited opportunities prevailing in the country. What most of them lack is capital with which to actualise their dreams. Many bankable project ideas die in people's cupboards or even in their dreams and minds due to lack of appropriate credit systems, institutions and infrastructure in the country.

Most rich people in the world have had to use "other people's money" in order to realise their dreams. They have had to borrow. Most rich people have prospered by wisely using borrowed money. Financial institutions in most developed countries charge interest rates lower than 10%. This encourages the borrower to utilise such facilities knowing pretty well that they can easily repay and at the same time make profit. Indeed the financial institutions aggressively compete to attract the clients to borrow. Incentives are also built in to encourage more people to borrow. Borrowed money carries with it the added challenge and responsibility requiring the borrower to repay the money back with interest.

When you borrow money to go into business, there is that constant reminder that the money is not yours and it has to be repaid. The borrower therefore indirectly benefits by the discipline and constant reminder that comes with it to ensure that the business is managed well so as to make profit so that the loan can be repaid. Even in Malawi, one would be pleasantly surprised to discover that almost all those powerful and rich people, owe the financial institutions significant amounts of money, or that they had to borrow in order to prosper.

Investment ideas have the potential to transform our country. They have potential to generate wealth, create jobs and import substitution. We will never know the ambitious dreams inherent in people's minds until innovative and appropriate credit systems and institutions are put in place. There is need to state a word of caution here. Credit systems and institutions need to be responsive and sensitive to the various needs of their *clientele*. Credit systems and institutions should cater for short, medium and long-term business needs. There are various credit instruments ranging from those for petty trading to cater for the needs of vendors. Other instruments cater for farmers who want to invest in farm inputs in order to enhance their productivity.

For agriculture production, the credit system needs to be responsive and sensitive to the unpredictability of weather as well as pest and disease infestation during the farming season. Other instruments should cater for credit requirements of those who want to invest in long-term production, tourist infrastructure and manufacturing ventures. Our country badly needs to develop the manufacturing and industrial base. We can never develop our country by converting every able-bodied Malawian into a vendor.

Credit systems should be flexible. Appropriate adjustments should easily be accommodated on the basis of need and justification. For instance, where need arises, additional credit should be made available in order to support farmers or other investors/borrowers in case of emergencies such as pest and disease infestation in order to help them protect their crops from total failure. This will enhance the farmer's ability to improve the yield but also his ability to repay the loan.

In cases where the farmer has not been able to harvest anything due to drought/floods, typhoons and other problems the credit institution should support the farmer plan and make adjustments accordingly. This will enhance the client confidence and would allow the farmers to position themselves strategically so that in the following year they can have adequate yield to service the credit for the two years. Where it is difficult to repay in one year the credit institution together with the client farmer should be able to work out an appropriate repayment schedule.

Other categories of credit requirements to stimulate economic development activities are small, medium and large-scale industrial investments. There are very good investment opportunities in the agro-processing sector in Malawi, for instance. This is in view of the diverse agricultural outputs. As highlighted earlier Malawi is an exporter of low value primary agricultural products but a net importer of manufactured high value goods, equipment and industrial raw materials. It is advisable for Malawi business people and foreign investors to consider the various investment opportunities in agro-processing in order to add value and ensure that processed or semi processed agricultural products are exported in order to add value thereby generate more foreign exchange for the country. In addition investment aimed at import-substitution should be considered more seriously.

There is also an untapped tourism industry in the country, which has gone untapped all these years as described above. The tourist industry is crying for investment resources. There is also need to invest in mineral and oil exploration. There are many unconfirmed reports that there are various quantities of mineral resources in the country. There have been many unsubstantiated reports also that there are oil fields in Lake Malawi and that there are gold, diamonds, uranium and other valuable mineral deposits in the country. There is need for aggressive exploration work to be undertaken. The Government and the donor community should follow these leads with a view to finance studies and exploration work to establish whether or not these deposits really exist within the borders of the country. If verified, these deposits provide tremendous investment opportunities. A conducive investment climate should also be established which encourages mobilisation of both offshore and internal investment resources.

Due to lack of appropriate credit systems and infrastructure, *katapila* dealers willingly fill the vacuum. These are unscrupulous business people whose conditions are unfavourable and enslave their clientele. Anyone who has had to borrow from these unscrupulous business people will tell you how hard it is. Not only are their interest rates exorbitant, ranging from 100 - 200% but failure to pay at the agreed time and amount automatically leads to compounding of the interest rate. Enforcement of the conditions is quite brutal and violent. The majority of the *katapila* barons are outlaws with dubious records. The poor people have no choice but to continue to patronise these unfriendly *katapila* barons due to unavailability of alternative sources of credit.

Unfortunately due to the extreme poverty in which most of the clients of this system find themselves, they are continuously indebted and the amounts owing keep growing in spite of their efforts to meet their repayments. Here are poor peasant farmers who have immediate needs for school fees, medical bills, farm inputs and many more. Yet they have no opportunities to borrow to cover their requirements from the official credit market. What are they supposed to do? The situation is critical and requires immediate attention.

In the 1970s and 80s the Government responded by establishing a number of institutions to lend money to the various categories of business entrepreneurs. Some of such institutions included the Small Enterprise Development of Malawi (SEDOM), African Businessmen Association (ABA), Investment and Development Bank (IndeBank), Malawi Development Corporation (MDC) among others. Unfortunately due to a number of reasons some of these institutions are now in name only. Not much is happening. Sadly most of these institutions have now been politicised. The lending systems and policies have over time become based on political patronage. Essentially, while criteria for lending is clearly set out, in practice loans are in many cases disbursed on the basis of political leaning of the client.

Availability of credit resources is of critical importance to facilitate the actualization of most people's dreams and goals. Even if one decided to start a small-scale vegetable garden to produce vegetables, there is need for some seed, fertilizer/manure, watering can and a hoe just to mention a few. All these require financial capital outlay. If the farmer does not have these basic requirements it may be difficult, though not impossible, to start the vegetable garden. The banking sector in Malawi is not responsive to the needs of the poor. The prevailing interest rates, in excess of 40%, are unrealistic. This is prohibitive. In addition, the lending institutions require collateral, which most poor people do not have.

Innovative ways need to be found to support the poor Malawian to achieve his/her goals. As has been repeatedly highlighted above, most poor people have powerful ideas, which if harnessed and supported could make a whole lot of a difference in their lives and the lives of their neighbourhoods and the country at large. If we are looking for one single action that will empower and enable the poor to overcome their poverty, there is need to make available credit facilities at affordable interest rate. Europe was rehabilitated and developed following the devastating Second World War by provisions of the Marshall Plan, which provided billions of dollars in grants and soft loans.

Today, Malawi is at a cross road where only the likes of the Marshall Plan can make a difference. In the absence of formal credit facilities and institutions that respond to the poors' circumstances, *katapila* barons continue to smile all the way to the bank and in the process overexploit the poor. For lack of alternative means and channels, the poor have no choice but to patronise the unfriendly *katapila* barons.

The Government and the rich Malawians both within the country and in Diaspora have a moral responsibility to ease this problem. If well managed the credit schemes have the potential to improve the lives of poor people in our country; create a bee hive of commercial activities in rural areas thereby stem the rural-urban migration; job creation; wealth creation; import-substitution and enhance export trade thereby generate foreign exchange. They also have a potential to revolve from one business person to another through a sustainable and well-planned repayment programme.

The focus for improving credit access to the poor including women and the youth should advocate high repayment rates and decreased administrative costs. Small loan sizes means higher costs per transaction. Group applications and economies of scale have potential to reduce the transaction costs. This will require that the rural poor organize themselves into groups, associations, co-operatives and other commodity based clubs/associations. Within the groups, individuals will prescribe precisely their take within the framework of the group credit. The credit resources will therefore be extended to the group and through peer pressure individual loan repayment will be ensured and enhanced.

Chapter Eleven

Take Action Now!

John F. Kennedy, the former American President challenged the American people not to ask: "what America can do for you but rather ask what you can do for America". Time has come for Malawians too to stop thinking in terms of what Malawi Government and the donor community will do for them but rather take action towards improving the lot of our people. This places the challenge right at each and every Malawian's doorstep. The challenge is so enormous and calls for all of us to take action. As highlighted earlier, the cumulative success stories, goals, wealth, accomplishments, dreams and values of individual Malawians are what define our national identity.

All your dreams, ideas and plans will come to naught unless you take action to implement them. The proof of the pudding is in the eating. As noted earlier, there are a lot of powerful ideas in the heads of the millions of Malawians that have potential to make a whole lot of a difference in the socio-economic development path of our country - if only these ideas were implemented. The sad thing is that most of your ideas are never implemented due to one reason or the other. The graves in Malawi are full of powerful ideas, which died in the heads of the fallen heroes. If only half of those ideas were given a chance, our country could have been different today. But let us not cry over spilt milk. There is nothing to be gained if we continue sulking. Let us all make renewed commitment to take action.

A multi-pronged approach is in order here with a view to rid ourselves of the scourge of poverty. The strategies should address economic, social, political and governance aspects of our lives. Nobody will do this for us. We must do this for ourselves. Even if there were other people out there ready to help us, the truth is that there is no dignity in handouts. Let us take full responsibility and be proud of our success. Indeed, good Samaritans can decide to walk away when they so wish. Sometimes when we need them most. There is pride, satisfaction and self-worth in seeing our achievements grow - no matter how small. Through our own sweat we must be committed to take hard and difficult decisions in order to turn our lives round.

You will never know how powerful and viable your ideas, dreams and plans are until you act on them. Even when your initial experiences are less successful, pick up the pieces, learn positive lessons from your mistakes and failures and move on to achieve success in your desired goals. Let us convert failures into success, negatives into positives. We should always have a positive attitude and faith that we are going to succeed. Most of us spend time and energy analyzing our powerful ideas in terms of cost-benefit analyses, profit and loss accounts, sensitivity analyses and risk analyses. Because of our negative attitudes we end up concluding that these investment ideas are not viable. We should endeavour to improve on this score. Rather than concluding that these beautiful investment ideas are not viable, we should find ways of fine-tuning the plans and ideas to make them viable and profitable.

Most of us also spend valuable time emphasizing our weaknesses and why we cannot succeed. Instead of emphasizing the assets, skills, talents, abilities and experiences we have, we spend time thinking about what we do not have. There is nothing to be gained by concentrating and focussing on what we do not have. We should capitalize on what we have and explore ways in which we can use what we have to make our world a better place to live. We should no longer emphasize on reasons like: Oh, I have inadequate money to actualise my dreams, the interest rate at the bank is too high, I am too young, I am too old, who will buy my products, the market is already flooded with the same goods and services and many self-defeatist tendencies. Rather than emphasize on the above negative aspects, you should take time to analyze, study, and seek advice and counsel from experts with a view to convert seemingly negative aspects into positive aspects. In addition let us emphasise our strengths rather than our weaknesses.

Procrastination is one major problem. This is the tendency to postpone action till tomorrow. There will always be reasons why today is not the right time to take action. But the right time to take action is today. Tomorrow is too late. If we keep on postponing till tomorrow, the activity will never be done because tomorrow will never come. We will be postponing for tomorrow, tomorrow and tomorrow till the activity will be forgotten. There are many instances when we have wanted to do something, but ended up postponing it. In the end we find that someone else took action and has succeeded beyond our wildest dreams. It could have been you enjoying that success and achievement if you had not postponed. That success should have been yours if you had taken action yesterday.

Let us not sulk or cry over already spilt milk. There are unlimited opportunities out there for us all. Let us take action today – not tomorrow. Malawi's economic reliance on export of primary agricultural commodities renders it particularly vulnerable to external shocks. Herein lies a challenge for you to act in bolstering our economy. Policy makers should ensure that they create an enabling environment for the rich Malawians both within and in Diaspora to invest in the country. Investments in productive activities and manufacturing industries will lead to more business activities, more jobs, wealth creation, export trade, import substitution and more foreign exchange earnings. In order for Malawi to carve out a niche in this competitive globalized world, we have to think seriously about converting our country from a consumer economy into a productive economy and from net importer into a net exporter. This is a tall order but one that can easily be achieved if all hands are on deck.

We must all take action to ease the suffering of the sick, old, widows, orphans, homeless and the poor. We must be compassionate and share the little we have with those who are in dire need. We must all take action in this noble cause. Let us take action to reduce our individual poverty. In the process we will also contribute to addressing the ills and needs of our communities and country. Let us identify those opportunities that lie within our reach. Let us capitalize on our passions, talents, skills and gifts to make a difference in our country.

We all have a lot of energy, enough to make a difference in the development of our country and our individual livelihoods. We can only appreciate the power of our imagination and dreams if we put them into action. As highlighted earlier, the twin sectors of agriculture and tourism should receive more attention as they hold the key to the country's development. More resources should be pumped into these sectors with a view to modernize and diversify our agricultural production. In agriculture particular attention should be placed on agro-business, agro-processing, export trade, irrigation, agriculture credit and research and development.

Tourism is largely a private sector activity. As long as the government creates an enabling environment the investors will come. Some of the issues to address include provision of adequate physical infrastructure such as roads, bridges, telecommunications, and water supplies. In addition issues of corruption, crime rate, political tolerance, good governance can improve the investors' willingness to come to invest in the country. Improvement of human capital through education and training should also receive particular attention. Furthermore deliberate effort should be made to stem the devastating HIV/Aids scourge, which is eating at the heart of the social fabric. Highly productive people and breadwinners are dying *en masse*. Aggressive action should be taken to control and reduce the rate of infection.

Chapter Twelve

The African Challenges

This chapter has been added as an after-thought. The readers are both present and future leaders of our land as well as continental leaders. They should be brought face to face with some of the realities of our contemporary world.

Africa is a very rich continent but inhabited by extremely poor people. This is a paradox of our time. There is pervasive poverty in the continent. More than 40% of Africans live below the poverty line. The problem is exacerbated by the high prevalence rates of HIV/Aids. So far 28 million people around the globe have died of HIV/Aids related infections. Currently about 30 million people are living with HIV or have AIDS. Of this number approximately 50% are in Africa. 60% of those infected in Africa are women. Considering the important role that women play in agricultural production in general and food production in particular the HIV/Aids pandemic is having an unprecedented impact on poverty and food security.

Recently, Prof. Victor Ngu, a renowned Cameroonian Doctor is said to have discovered a cure for HIV/Aids. He has invented a vaccine called Vanhixax. It is reported that scientific evidence shows that the vaccine is curing HIV/Aids. The powerful international media is shunning this discovery. The discovery by Prof. Ngu is real good news for Africa. One wonders why there is no aggressive publicity of this good news. Indeed there have been other reported discoveries in this regard in Malawi, Nigeria, Uganda and other countries. Within the framework of NEPAD, consideration should be given to support all these various doctors to deepen their research with hope to find lasting cure for HIV/Aids. The HIV/Aids pandemic is most rampant in Africa. This places the onus on African leaders, scientists and traditional healers to find cure as quickly as possible.

Africa has a lot of natural resources including abundant mineral resources, wildlife, water, forests, crude oil and very hard working and resilient people. Some of the mineral resources include gold, diamonds, uranium, gemstones, iron, copper and vermiculite just to name a few. The continent also boasts a diversity of culture, traditional dances, ethnic groups, languages, foodstuffs and many more. The inhabitants of the African Continent are yet to wake up, open their eyes and realize the phenomenal wealth available just under their feet. The amount of wealth in Africa is massive. We need to sharpen our imaginative and perceptive facilities in order to be able to tap from the abundant resources that are within reach. One of the legacies of colonialism are the borders created between and/or among what had always been one people. In addition to the boundaries, the colonial legacy left a divided continent on account of languages – Anglophones, Francophones, Lusophones etc. This does have its associated problems on communication and interaction among the peoples. It is time we dismantled these imaginary boundaries and also enhance intra-African trade. Let us encourage more trade among African countries. The prices for our primary agricultural commodities are determined very far away from the production sites and in the process, African farmers lose out. The more we develop continental trading partnerships, some of the problems associated with trans-ocean trade can be done away with.

Africa has numerous challenges. One of the major challenges is the conversion of the abundant natural resources endowment into goods and services that are required on the international market with a view to meet both domestic as well as export markets. This can generate wealth. The lack of such industrial development generates joblessness, desperation and poverty. Unfortunately our leaders do not seem to take this issue seriously.

Africa is a net importer of goods and services. They are consumer economies. Apart from a few countries, which have significant manufacturing industries, the bulk of the countries in Africa import almost everything ranging from food, fuel, industrial raw material, equipment, farm machinery, cars, computers, jewellery, paper, pencils, toilet tissue, beer, wine, sewing needles, matches, sickles, bicycles and much more. We cannot even manufacture sewing needles - what a shame! Unfortunately the poor African also has learnt to enjoy exotic imported goods and services. One would have expected the poor to have appetites for basic and locally manufactured goods. This is not to be. This state of affairs deepens the poverty status in Africa even further.

There is need to create an enabling environment for democracy, good governance, peace, food security, industrial development, export trade and economic growth and development in Africa. In addition there is need for an internally funded "Marshal Plan" to support rehabilitation and development of requisite physical and economic infrastructure throughout Africa. The rich African countries should consider establishing a fund through which poor nations can access development resources at concessional interest rates, including grants.

There is need to harness Africa's economic success stories and adapt technological breakthroughs to the African environment. There is an urgent need for African Governments to provide adequate funds for research and development to spearhead industrial innovation and development. In addition Africa should move quickly to make necessary changes that will allow Africans to travel freely within the continent. The requirement for Africans to have visa when travelling on their own continent is not only laughable but unnecessary – this is the 21st century.

Although on paper African countries are independent sovereign states, it is clear that the developed world, international financial institutions and the World Trade Organisation are the ones that have the clout. They can decide the economic path for us. They can even determine when a particular African Country should devalue its currency, retrench a certain percent of its civil service, introduce multiparty democracy, and privatize parastatal organizations or whatever else they may consider to be good for us. We do not have the power anymore to determine our own developmental agenda. How did the situation get this far and this bad?

In some countries they are even involved in providing financial support to opposition parties in some African countries, with a view to support regime change. The west is in charge of African affairs by proxy. In the history of Africa there have been powerful and progressive leaders. They have all met their fate orchestrated either openly or clandestinely supported by the west. Examples abound.

The west thrives on divide and rule and manipulative tactics. But such tactics can only prevail when some greedy and corrupt African leaders cooperate. Where an African President is progressive and has strategies towards African self-reliance and when such policies do not favour the west, they do not hesitate to take action "in the interest of democracy." Africans need to be careful and take necessary steps in the interest of Africa's emancipation and development.

It is increasingly clear that most of our leaders are greedy, corrupt and connive with the west. In this regard, they take selfish decisions in line with the interests of the west knowing pretty well that such decisions are not for the economic benefit of their people. In many cases such decisions bring petty personal gain to the leader and their circle of friends and sycophants while enslaving millions of citizenry.

We must continue to search for leaders who have the welfare of our continent at heart who can lead us through the mess to socio-economic development, democracy, peace and prosperity. In most countries what we have are rulers. What we need are leaders. There is a mismatch between what we have and what we need for Africa's peace, democracy and economic development and growth.

New Africa (NA) Magazine, Issue No. 414 of January 2003, provides some interesting reading about the Bilderburg Group, a secretive and informal grouping of powerful western corporate and political figures which meets every year to strategically map out international financial and economic deals. At such meetings they build consensus on how political and corporate affairs should be handled and managed. In addition, there is yet another business forum called Trilateral Commission where powerful western business people, politicians and bankers meet to map out strategies on how world business affairs should be conducted.

The absence of African representation is quite conspicuous. No African is allowed anywhere near the venues of such meetings. This is how international business deals are struck in the 21st century. In Africa we seem to be living in the 18th century, while being surrounded by 21st century players and stakeholders. Is it therefore surprising that Africa is being left out? Is it surprising that all deals cut out at such fora are to the detriment of Africa? Our African Leaders need to wake up and be part of the world order or choose to perish

Most African political leaders are extremely corrupt and continue to shamelessly loot their countries' hard earned wealth. The poor peasants work hard under the hot sun in order to eke out a living. They dutifully pay tax from the meagre resources. Yet the taxes paid by these poor people end up in the politicians' pockets and their foreign bank accounts. This is not only sad but also criminal. When our countries borrow from the international lending institutions for developmental requirements, in many cases only a small proportion of the resources are used for the intended purposes. The bulk of it is either looted or used for political agenda including procurement of votes and vote rigging.

The bulk of wealth in the African countries ends up in the fat bank accounts of their leaders in developed countries. One gets the impression that there is conspiracy among the developed world to keep developing countries, particularly in Africa downtrodden. For how can they accept the inflows of clearly looted money into their banks without question? Why can't they say no. Why can't they send such looted money back to the countries of origin to finance much-needed development projects? Arguably, the developed countries make a lot of money on the looted money, in the form of interest charges when such money is lent out to the same poor countries from where it had been looted. In addition the African leaders pay a lot of money to have their looted money hidden safely.

The African elite and political class should be discouraged from looting. On the contrary they should be encouraged to invest hard-earned money at home. Of course we should strive to choose honest leaders. We need to establish a conducive investment climate where all our brothers and sisters who have money can begin to save in the continent. Our money saved in Africa will generate wealth, jobs, and contribute to poverty alleviation.

Indeed some of the money African governments borrow from the developed countries may actually be our own money, which our dear politicians have looted and stashed away in these western capitals. If our African leaders refrained from the habit of looting, Africa would be a different place. Then and only then will Africa have adequate resources for its development plans. We may not even need to borrow.

The fact that children of our political leaders go to school abroad helps to explain why they care less about the quality of our education system and institutions. The fact that the politicians themselves fly out to first class hospitals abroad also helps to explain why they do not pay much attention to improve the health services in Africa. Furthermore because they travel by plane and visit parts of their countries by helicopter they may not be familiar with or care about the gaping potholes on our roads. They should all be encouraged to patronize our hospitals and send their children to our schools. Only then shall we see some significant improvement in much of our public services.

There are incessant civil conflicts of varying ferocity in Africa - in Rwanda, Burundi, Democratic Republic of Congo (DRC), Liberia, Sierra Leone, Sudan, Angola Cote d'Ivoire, Central African Republic (CAR) and many other places. Invariably these countries are rich in natural resources and have great potential for economic development. The civil wars leave behind a trail of infrastructure destruction, loss of life and property, destitution and need for financial support for reconstruction and rehabilitation. Who provides the needed resources? Who provides the war machinery - guns, bullets, helicopters, tanks, gunships, ammunitions, tanks, rocket launchers and all the regalia that go with war? Who provides war relief and emergency support after the war and carnage?

The civil wars in Africa provide the west with opportunities for wealth and job creation. They use the same wars to provide humanitarian support in terms of grants and loans. Our civil conflicts also provide the west with the opportunity to test their newly invented guns and war machines. Furthermore the civil wars provide them with market outlet for their manufacturing industry for war machines, and equipment.

All Africa needs is stop the senseless fighting. The resources we use to buy guns and ammunition could then be used for development. It is not a straightforward matter because the west has an interest to see the continuation of fighting, confusion and mayhem. After all they make a few dollars through the African conflicts. Africa should be united otherwise they can employ various tactics of divide and rule to perpetuate the fighting and civil wars in Africa. Very simple internal or border conflicts in Africa are fanned into full-fledged conflicts so that they can sell their guns and ammunition. African leaders should open their eyes a bit wider in order to be able to see these strategies. It is high time we put a stop to this madness and stupidity.

Globalization provides an opportunity for a few rich people and corporate bodies to amass wealth and get richer while the majority get poorer. The poor African cotton, banana or vegetable farmer for instance, cannot favourably compete on the international market with the multinational banana producing conglomerates, especially when such conglomerates are beneficiaries of billions of dollars of subsidies from the western capitals. The west provides hundreds of billions of dollars each year in subsidies to its farmers. Yet the international financial institutions and the donor community do not want to hear about the peasant African farmer being provided with any subsidy.

The donor community argue that it is not sustainable and that the African countries cannot afford it. This state of affairs has led to non-profitability of African agriculture. Because the poor farmers can no longer afford farm inputs agricultural productivity and production has declined over time. Even after applying all the farm inputs the prices for agriculture products which are also determined by international institutions make it is extremely difficult for our farmers to break-even. This situation is encouraging most farmers to leave the rural areas in search for remunerative employment. In addition, we are increasingly witnessing dumping of low quality and cheap products from the west into our African markets.

Only a decade ago, almost all African countries were self-sufficient in food requirements. Now most African countries import the bulk of their food requirements. The African farmer cannot afford the farming inputs, fertilizers, seed, pesticides, fungicides and farm implements due to the removal of subsidies. The financial institutions also do not provide credit to the poor peasant farmers because they have no collateral. The end result is that agricultural production in Africa is no longer profitable.

At the end of the Second World War, Germany and most parts of Europe were destroyed. America provided billions of Dollars under the Marshall Plan for reconstruction and rehabilitation. The resources provided under the Marshall Plan enabled Europe to recover economically as well as to rehabilitate the destroyed infrastructure and industries. The support included grants and loans. Today Africa is in dire need of development resources but developed countries have conspired to keep Africa perpetually poor. They do not want to provide a Marshall Plan for Africa. On the contrary, the conditions for aid to African Countries seem to be designed to perpetuate poverty.

The developed countries are therefore not sympathetic to the African cause. To sort out African developmental challenges we, Africans must be prepared to sweat it out and make necessary sacrifices. In spite of massive aid resources received so far nothing has changed. We must change course. We must also accept that the worst enemy to the African cause happens to be the African himself/herself! There is a big challenge here to make the African more friendly to the African cause.

The New Partnership for Africa's Development (NEPAD) initiative is but one forum through which Africa can take its destiny in its own hands. It is sad that the initial framework has been mooted by a few African leaders who have had to take it to the G8 Meeting for endorsement. The worst aspect is that the NEPAD framework has been endorsed by the G8 Summit before being debated and fully accepted by Africans themselves. Why should we need the G8 endorsement for Africa's developmental framework? In addition, the plan requires resources to the tune of US$64 billion per year and Africa intends to raise this magnitude of resources from the G8! Good luck. The G8 countries are going to monitor and supervise the implementation of the NEPAD plan of action.

The G8 countries have so far pledged only $1 billion per year for 6 years - a total of $6 billion. It will take 64 years for NEPAD to get its full compliment of annual resource needs at the current rate of commitments. This has to be contrasted with the more than $120 billion rescue plan, which the IMF and the US put together in 1997 to rescue Asian economies during the worst Asian economic crisis. In 2002 Europe and the US raised hundreds of billions of dollars for rebuilding and rehabilitation of Afghanistan following the devastating war that was waged to oust the Taliban led Government there. And more recently hundreds of billions of dollars have been pledged and disbursed by America and Britain for security, rehabilitation and reconstruction of Iraq following the ouster of Saddam Hussein. For NEPAD, the entire developed world can only pledge US$6 billion to cover a period of 6 years – that is US$1 billion per year for the entire continent of 53 countries. The message is clear for those with ears to hear and eyes to see!

The foregoing tells a complex story - the relative importance of Africa on the geo-political affairs of the world. The African leaders behave as if nothing is happening and as though everything is all right. The fact of the matter is that everything is not all right! In fact the approach adopted by NEPAD in its bid to raise fiscal resources is totally wrong. Africa has come of age. Africa has the resource base more than enough to finance its development programme without the need to depend on anybody. Africa has the capacity to monitor its own activities without the G8's support and supervision. Indeed Africa also has the expertise and capability for its development programmes and to monitor its affairs. Africa needs to mobilize internal resources for the NEPAD plan of action.

All African meetings and conferences are freely attended by the west without any hindrance. We should learn from the west by ensuring that some of our meetings should be conducted without the attendance of non-Africans. The west has some secretive fora to which no

African representative is admitted. Why should we allow the west free access to all our meetings? There is no justification - we also need to have our own secretive fora at which only African issues are discussed for the consumption of African ears and eyes. As has been repeated, Africa has the resource base and capacity required for her development. All that is required is a bit of perceptive and imaginative thinking, strategic planning, organization, and mobilization of internal resources. Africa must start to think and strategize. The Western countries spend time and effort to think how to keep Africa in disunity and perpetuate our poverty so that they can continue to exploit our differences and poverty.

Africa's poverty and problems are a multi billion-dollar industry. Yet Africa is still sleepwalking as if everything is all right. The most dangerous state of affairs is when one does not know that s/he has a problem. It would appear our leaders do not realize the seriousness of our geo-political problems and isolation. Africa has a lot of resources and we do not need the west to organize a Marshall Plan for us.

Remember - every problem, no matter how big, has a soft spot. Where there is will there is way. If there is political will we can mobilize internal resources and those of our brothers and sisters in Diaspora for the African homemade Marshall Plan. Africans must open their sleepy eyes and start thinking strategically.

What has been highlighted in this chapter is only the tip of a mammoth iceberg. From the little that has been highlighted, it is clear that there are global challenges that Africa has to contend with. The African Union (AU) has lots of homework to do in this regard to justify its relevance. It should not turn into yet another talk shop. The first major challenge is to effectively integrate our economies into one big continental economy. Africa has about 700 million people. This provides a big market for our infantile industrial products, agricultural products, mineral products and many others.

The intra-Africa trade should be of primary importance. There is need for strategic thinking and approach to international relations and diplomacy. The colonial borders should be brought down. Africans should never require a passport to move from one African country to another. Africa has had a raw deal in all its dealings with the western capitals. Time has come when some sober analysis and thinking should guide our destiny and developmental path.

Success and wealth are indeed around the corner – if you have a burning desire for success and wealth. If you also have belief, hope and faith in yourself and your goal. You need to use your imaginative and perceptive mind. You need to use your God-given talents, skills, gifts, manual dexterity and mind. You should learn to step out of the crowd – nothing much is achieved in a mass rally. Get out of your comfort zone and discover a whole new world in front of you with unlimited opportunities.

You require some imagination, perceptive mind and a detailed plan. If you face setbacks and problems, do not give up – hang in there! Those problems you face are only temporary and are supposed to be used as stepping stones and your ladder to success. Problems and stumbling blocks are only meant to separate boys from men. I hope you are no longer a boy. It may help to pause and ask yourself some questions – Who are you? Why are you here on earth? What are your special skills, talents, gifts, and attitudes? What are your goals, objectives, and purpose in life? What difference can you bring in your own life as well as in the lives of your neighbours? What are the next steps you need to take in order to make a difference in your life? Are you willing to make some changes in your life, attitude, lifestyle, perceptions, imagination, thought processes in order to achieve success in your life?

I truly wish you the very best as you work hardest in order to actualise your dreams .... Good luck.

www.ingramcontent.com/pod-product-compliance
Lightning Source LLC
Chambersburg PA
CBHW020006290326
41935CB00007B/329